A Horse's Thought

A Journey into Honest Horsemanship

A Horse's Thought

A Journey into Honest Horsemanship

Tom Moates

SPINNING SEVENS
PRESS

New edition created April 2010
Designed by Chris Legg

Cover photo by Kathy Baker

Dedication

This book is dedicated to Harry Whitney, whose quiet, patient, unfailing ways with horses truly inspire.

Contents

Foreword

A lot of people are doing just enough to get by these days. Few are really committed to what they do as a career or even as a spouse or parent. Tom Moates is not one of these. He is committed. The kind of commitment that has him sitting and sleeping in a chair at the hospital for days and weeks that turned into months as his wife, Carol, went through two, yes two, liver transplants. This was of course driven by his commitment as a husband. Tom has this same kind of commitment to his writing/journalism. Once he made the addicting move to involvement with horses there is the same kind of commitment to becoming the best horseman he could be. Combine a commitment to understanding horses with a commitment to good journalism and you have a man on the edge of needing to be committed (if you know what I mean... institutionalized).

It is his commitment to accuracy and truth that come across in his writing. Tom takes great care to get "it" right. Tom and I have spent many hours on the phone going over concepts and philosophies of horsemanship. Still he continues to check if he is correct in fear of misleading his readers. Where he is in this horsemanship journey is ever changing as it is for each of us. Tom can only share the truth and understanding of the horse from where he is and his experience at this point in time. I am sure you will find each of these essays/chapters entertaining and enjoyable reading. More importantly though I hope you find them thought provoking, as each chapter deals with an individual concept of horsemanship. Tom isn't trying to tell you "how to" do something but rather sharing a thought or philosophy in a way to stimulate your own thinking.

The more people think about the concepts that apply to horsemanship the closer they get to a oneness with their horse. No one exercise or "how to" move applies to all horses and all situations but there are overarching concepts that can bring some clarity to a multitude of situations with your horse. If these things do not come through clearly from this book that is understandable. But I assure you, it is not from lack of commitment on the part the author. Thank you Tom for your commitment to horses, to horsemanship, to honesty and correctness, to journalism, but most importantly, to us your readers.

Harry Whitney
October 2008

Acknowledgments

Without Harry Whitney, this book could not be. I must thank him for tolerating my antics, my constant inquiries, and for being a great friend. I am eternally grateful for all he has done for me, and that reaches way beyond what's found between these covers. He also took the great image of me which accompanies the author's information, and I am very pleased he agreed to allow me to use it in this book, and for providing other images from his collection. You may find out more about Harry at www.HarryWhitney.com.

Many of these pages are already dedicated to him and his work, so I'll leave my thanks to him at that, and go to some others who are more behind the scenes....

Emily Kitching deserves a huge thanks. She was the first to publish my horsemanship essays which run in her magazine, *Eclectic-Horseman*, and she continues to publish the series from which some of this book appeared originally in print. Emily and her husband, Steve Bell, design and run my website, www.tommoates.com, and I could not be more pleased with the simplicity of that arrangement! They take care of everything, and always seem to get into the webpage design just what I want, even though I can't really explain it to them before hand.

Emily and Steve are taking care of many distribution concerns for this book, and I enjoy seeing real people, like them, with a real family business, be involved with any project I produce. I greatly appreciate their willingness to take on some of the off-the-beaten-path articles and endeavors I bring their way. I am deeply grateful for the support from them that has made much of this book possible. You can find out more at www.eclectic-horseman.com.

Holly Clanahan and Becky Newell, editors at the American Quarter Horse Association magazine, *America's Horse*, deserve a huge thank you for supporting this book. They printed several essays that are included in here in various forms, and have been extremely supportive of my writing in general. I appreciate their interest in allowing me to introduce the AQHA membership to a little of Harry Whitney's work as a clinician. I really value their input and continuing support, as well as that of all the staff I know at the AQHA, who are great friends. For more go to www.aqha.com.

Many of the photographs in this book were taken by two talented photographers, Terry McCoy and Pam Talley Stoneburner. I've known Terry for many years, and recently met Pam. Their abilities to capture visuals of some of what I try to discuss in this book are extremely helpful, and they are very generous to allow me to use their excellent images. Their contributions are greatly appreciated.

Thanks to Rainey Houston for again allowing me to use some of her photography in this book. Her images of me and our horses have been extensively published, and have accompanied some of the material from this book in magazine excerpts.

None of this would have happened or even been remotely possible without the support and constant input from my wife, Carol. Her opinions, photographs, editorial skills, and tolerance of my rather zealous writing and horsemanship endeavors are completely entwined with all I accomplish. Not to mention she really introduced me to horses. So many, many thanks to her for all that went into helping bring this book to life.

Introduction

Harry Whitney never yet agreed to write a book or make
a video. It isn't, however, for lack of opportunity or interest in the
horse world. There may be several reasons for his decision. One
I know for sure is that horsemanship is such a difficult, nebulous,
and vast area to discuss, that no static answers exist to questions so
many people have about their horses—so Harry wonders how could
he publish anything that's bound to be misinterpreted or that he
might himself feel differently about in a little while after he's learned
something new?

I know the feeling. My first book, *Discovering Natural Horsemanship*, accurate as it is for the beginner that I was at the time trying to figure things out in the world of horses, contains nowhere near the amount of insight into working with horses that this book illustrates. That memoir account of being a beginner is still valid (thank goodness), and possesses stories of insight both fun and educational to some extent. As far as reading an account about really getting something going with a horse, though...it can't even come close to this book. I lacked the years of experience and exposure to the teachings of a capable mentor like Harry Whitney required to create an account of more serious discoveries. Far deeper levels of working with horses in a truly meaningful way are found in this more recent work. Hopefully, I'll continue to work and grow and increase my equine understanding and the future will provide yet more advanced written insights from my mis-adventures. We'll see.

Knowing Harry's position on the reluctance to write books or produce videos only increases my respect for his clearly authentic personal approach to provide the closest thing to truth he can at any given time to best help folks and horses. It is certainly not the most profitable trail for a gifted clinician to take. So far, however, it is the one he knows is right for himself, and when convinced of that in any aspect of life, Harry is unwavering.

Harry's present view of producing recorded accounts of his ways may or may not change in the future, but right now I can tell you it makes me incredibly honored that Harry agreed to allow me to present a small window into some of his work in these pages. Enormous gravity and responsibility tugs on me when I document onto the page my experiences and how Harry influenced them. I work double overtime to try and make certain not only am I pleased with the written results regarding my horsemanship illuminations, but that his work is presented as it affected me as accurately to the reader as possible. I hope this work does justice to Harry's abilities, and the insightful help thus afforded me so far.

Those of us who already know, follow, and respect Harry should easily recognize his words and ways as they unfolded in my personal experiences shared in these chapters. Those who as yet haven't been to a Harry clinic hopefully catch a glimpse of how helpful, fun, and really profound the experience of his teaching can be. Harry still travels a regular circuit each year, so go check out his website and see what the schedule looks like (www.harrywhitney.com).

With any luck I'll see you there, along with many of the other usual suspects you'll come to know before you're finished reading this book.

Mostly, when summed up, I hope some of my work helps others get along better with their horses. Not that there are answers in here per se, as I'll repeat over and over, but I hope what comes across is rather that cornerstone of Harry's teaching: to begin to consider things from the horse's point of view.

I desire for this book to help folks find the right questions that in turn lead to the answers that are right for their horses. I still hope that for myself, to tell you the truth! So, good luck to us, and may we always prioritize taking the time to go work with our horses.

Tom Moates
October 2008

Note Regarding
Second Edition

I'm very pleased to present the new edition of *A Horse's Thought, A Journey Into Honest Horsemanship*. I'd like to give a special thanks to Chris Legg, whose brilliant graphics design work is responsible for the completely revamped cover and layout. Editing and changes of the new edition were kept to a minimum. It is not my desire to alter the original book, but the opportunity arose with a change of publishers to make improvements on some important issues that troubled me in the earlier hard and soft back versions— so I jumped at the chance.

Tom Moates

April 2010

Chapter 1

(Rainey Houston)

A Horse's Thought

"Hanging between two reins is a thought," I heard Harry
Whitney say.

The statement proved profound for me. Profound in its truth
and simplicity. It pretty much wrecked everything I'd been working on
for a couple of years with horses.

Harry Whitney. *(Pam Talley Stoneburner)*

Traveling the trail to develop the best relationship possible with horses, and actively attempting to achieve this goal, it is pretty hard to avoid catch phrases. They're usually funny, sexy, and often delivered with perfect timing for just the right affect on the grandstand. Some are even trademarked (!). I bet by this time I'd heard just about every one out there.

This was different.

First of all, it wasn't delivered for an impressive effect the way some throw out a golden nugget of wisdom previously choreographed, proof-tested on audiences, and perfected to make the orator seem like a horsemanship ninja to the less experienced. Not that Harry isn't a ninja, he is...he's just not a rock star ninja. Anyway, the words came from his own genuine interest and desire to help us onlookers understand that nebulous world of horsemanship as he lives, sees, and works it. The statement attempted to reveal a piece of understanding that had occurred to him uniquely through his own intense desire to reach horses, and to get them to a better space within themselves when interacting with humans.

Second of all, even in less than ideal weather, clinic goers worked horses with Harry. More typically before this experience, I attended clinics in big fancy indoor arenas. Not that we wouldn't have used such a space just then if one had been available; believe me, we would have. But, by contrast, some of the horsemanship clinic venues I'd seen had a multitude of booths for shopping on the concourse, and staffs so vast that they sometimes even included a music d.j. trained to synchronize tunes for certain interactive moments between clinician and audience for a big effect. That all suddenly smacked as being less than authentic to me in retrospect, and less about the horse, as I watched my first Harry Whitney clinic.

At this time, Harry sat on a horse with cold drizzle beading up on his glasses, even under his cowboy hat. The damp cowboy paid more attention at that moment to the horse's immediate needs than to what the audience was up to. The only reason I even heard what he said as he concentrated on that horse at that moment was because he had a wireless microphone that fed a speaker that was close to me, wrapped in a plastic garbage bag on a tripod, also dripping wet.

Tom works on leading Niji's thought. *(Terry McCoy)*

This damp chilly day was one of my first in the middle of the Arizona dessert. I would not have guessed I'd be huddling around the open door of an old Franklin woodstove with several other folks. The fire crackled and projected a warmth farther than I would have guessed to be outside as it was, positioned between a large shipping container used as a tack and feed storage room and an awesome round pen made from new shiny green panels with a groomed sandy footing. A smokestack went up ten feet to carry the smoke up and out away from the area.

The audience was attentive, but wrapped in whatever layers had been brought along on the trip. There was no reason for clinician or audience to be suffering the elements there except to try and get better with horses. No slick extra entertainment. No shopping opportunities. No prizes. No big earth shattering momentous visual change in someone's horse every five minutes. Just the genuine drive to make each moment count towards improving the understanding that might make a permanent dent in our brains and provide new equestrian understanding that sticks.

"Hanging between those reins is a thought," Harry reiterated, looking straight down the horse's neck from the saddle where he sat, concentrating on just how to explain what he meant to eight of us sitting there. "It's not too hard to send or lead or direct a thought."

Of course...that's it! I saw it right then. "Send, lead, or direct..." the key was right there. Why hadn't I seen it before? "Send," "lead," and "direct" are very different verbs than the one I had based all of my attempts to find the best way to work with horses before...which had been to "drive."

I realized for the first time how such subtle differences in approach and meaning created very significant consequences for horses. And this was just the first layer of the onion beginning to peel back.

I recorded in my notes that night what Harry had said. Then I wrote some other commentary which says that the point of the lesson is that if you have a horse's thought, you have the feet. If you have the feet, then you have the horse.

Classic Harry Whitney teachings, I've since come to understand, always include two basic truths: asking how the horse feels about things inside himself, and that you should learn to ask a horse to send his thoughts to places before thinking about having his body go there. This is the key to the universe, pretty much. Before this, I was sure the key was in "pressure and release."

I should go ahead and confuse the issue right away and say that pressure and release is in a sense still the basis for getting a horse's thought with you. But, I understood from that point on that it isn't simply mechanical in nature, as I only had seen it presented before.

For example, I never saw Harry poke a horse to get the "pressure" side of that equation. Many other clinicians I'd been around focus mainly on poking horses, then releasing the poke. Swatting the horse with a swinging end of a rope every time they asked for forward. Driving the horse forward in a round corral by smacking their chaps with a coiled rope all the time. Working with a horse's thought, when done right, does not require poking, driving, or swatting a horse busily. One leads the horse's mind, and the horse moves himself without the crude need to be mechanically convinced.

This idea permeates what Harry teaches, and likewise what I now try to get going with horses. To even have a chance to "get it," one must from the onset of digging deeper into this world of horsemanship be acquainted with the concept of the horse's thought. The very foundation of the best work with horses begins when we lead them by guiding their thoughts, not when we drive their bodies. It must be the essence of our approach right when we start to work with horses, or we are failing them before we even get anything done.

If we aren't building better feelings and actions in our horses, then unfortunately, we're doing the opposite: dulling them, bringing about trouble, and quite frankly teaching them the opposite of what we hope to achieve.

To lead horses well and truly have them on board following us willingly, even enthusiastically and with a sense of purpose, there is no room for them to feel they are fleeing from us, mentally or physically. To lead a horse is a very different situation than to cause to the horse to escape from pressure we inflict. When we make a request of a horse, the horse should be able to answer it without hesitation, but not in a hurried way. Calm confidence and contentment to respond to our requests without any wavering is the goal. It is attainable. It is the ultimate equestrian/human relationship. It also comes with tremendous responsibility. Once we get a horse's confidence to follow us, we had better have somewhere to go! Otherwise, why have we bothered the poor horse? That is a kind of lie, and we should exercise the foresight to be ready to have purpose in our riding when the horse breaks through and gets on board with us mentally.

The horse is often committed to his own thought, even when this mental condition causes him trouble and anxiety. Our changing this pattern and leading the horse into a new direction should always be to prove to the horse that there is another way that will make him feel better, as well as being more useful to us. It can be rather difficult to break that equine line of thinking at first, and gain his attention, let alone confidence.

Oddly, sometimes to the untrained eye, getting a horse's attention and penetrating his thoughts so he can have a chance to see

Sandy and Big Easy getting turned out at Harry's place in Arizona.
(Tom Moates)

ours, looks a lot like driving him. There is, however, a huge difference. This distinction is in timing, intention, feel, and approach. Driving the body sets the stage for future resentment, anxiety, and continuing troubled feelings. Leading the horse's thought brings about an unfolding of improvement, with a calming affect, increasing confidence, and a lightness unattainable if the horse withholds them, or directs them somewhere other than with us.

"Hanging between two reins is a thought," Harry said. If we can visualize that, then what follows naturally is the understanding that those reins, never ever turn the head or the horse. Rather, they simply steer the horse's thought.

Once established, one can ever so gently ask the horse to think around to the right with just a finger on the rein, then watch his head turn as he thinks around that way. No bracing in the neck. No head popping up in opposition to the rein. No. You're not manipulating the flesh in any physical way. There is never a need for a more severe bit. Why? Because all the rein does is present a slight suggestion. If that horse is with you, his brain understands the lightest request and he is ready to commit to the suggestion whole heartedly and bring his own body along too.

If you don't have this, then your horse isn't feeling okay inside with the situation, and it's time to ask some new questions and try to understand some new answers.

Chapter 2

(Harry Whitney Collection)

Deconstruction

Honestly, when I traveled to Salome, Arizona from Virginia for two weeks to learn from clinician Harry Whitney, I expected to build on the solid foundation I'd worked for several years to lay up towards a better way of working with horses. I figured the base was solid. After all, I'd obsessively worked to read, watch, attend, and practice all I could towards learning this Better Way with horses, call it what you will. This opportunity I figured would be the beginnings of the structure to be framed on top of that base. But...that's not what happened.

What I got was just the opposite. I got deconstructed. I got those foundation stones torn down before the first sill was placed upon them, and a whole new floor plan presented to me.

And, to make it all the worse, I lived in awareness of it the whole time. Just like the sudden new understanding of working with a horse's thought versus how much I had been just driving my horses' bodies around. I knew it was happening to me because I participated in it. It--this deeper understanding I sought--actually began to make sense, but I had to face the grueling reality that I must be willing to let go of much of what I brought to the Arizona desert with me.

How do I tell this story? It is one of those that is about the intangibles, like feel. How do you put the invisible into words?

No one can possibly say it better than my mare, Sokeri, said it to me the day I got back from Arizona. Soke (pronounced So-kay), for short, had been with me for several years. She was my first horse, and from the first day she came home I worked with her in the "natural horsemanship" ways. I only had worked just a little with horses before her, so everything in the horse world was new to me.

She came "broke," which is a good way to put it since she was completely shut down and accustomed to being dominated. I explored natural horsemanship from a variety of sources, and that whole beginning is shared in my book, Discovering Natural Horsemanship, "A Beginner's Odyssey," if you care to read the gory details of the complete novice trying to sort out getting better with horses. I finished that book on a Friday, and left the very next morning at 3 a. m. for

Harry's. The timing turned out to be incredibly poignant.

All the work I did with horses leading up to Arizona was progress of a kind. The mare opened up in time, and we worked through many technical details. I learned tons from all kinds of sources and experiences. Pressure and release was working for us pretty well from the ground and the saddle. I could send her around the round pen, changing speeds and then back off the pressure and bring her in to me. The signs from her indicated to me in my mind that we were getting on great. She listened fine. There were still some problems, and trouble would resurface in areas I had already cleared out, which I thought was weird, but it seemed clear that our relationship was fine and she trusted me.

Then I watched Harry for ten hours a day for two weeks. What startled me at first was what he didn't do. The first day I watched Harry in the round pen, I could hardly believe how little he did at times that day. I was pretty dumbfounded. I'd seen a range of clinicians, and always they seemed to be driving a horse around the round pen, whether at liberty or working on lead with some exercise, but always busy—often Harry just waited. One horse provides a great example of what I mean. The gelding was trotting circles around the fence of the round corral, nose in the air. Harry just stood there summing-up the situation, then he made the big move...he slapped the end of a lead rope on his chap. The horse looked at him for a second, then went back to what he was up to before.

"This horse's thought is out there," Harry said, pointing out that the horse's eyes, ears, and mind were directed out of the round pen. "I'm just gonna say, 'hey, it's better over here [that was what he meant with the simple slap of the chap with the rope].' This horse doesn't feel good inside. That's why he thinks it is necessary to run around and try to get over there. He thinks it's out there, but really it's over here with me. It'll feel better to him over here. He'll figure it out."

And, oddly enough, with nothing more than a series of slaps on his chaps (and light ones at that) the horse began to look his way more and more. Then, the horse slowed to a walk along the fence. Before long, he left the fence and circled closer to Harry. Finally, the horse stopped and decided to see how it felt by Harry, where he got his nose stroked and neck rubbed.

This took awhile, and I could see the chap slaps were well timed to points where the horse was leaving with his thought. Thus, the whole series of slaps just brought the horse's attention back in towards him. All together they amounted to a simple conversation, reinforcing what Harry wanted to say to the horse. It was startling to me at that moment, because every other clinician I'd seen would have had this horse standing there by him in less time, but would have accomplished it with way more pressure.

I'd never seen a horse brought around to a person with such a gentle touch. I'd seen horses driven around a round pen a hundred times with coiled rope slapping against chaps, or flag whipping around. Even if done gently, it was still done in a way that drove the horse. It wasn't so with Harry in this instance, and it created a whole new reference point on the soft end of the pressure spectrum for me that I never knew existed. He wasn't driving the horse at all. He was just standing there. I don't remember ever being so fascinated to sit and watch somebody just stand there! But, the way it slowly unfolded was completely the horse's decision to move or not, and at what speed. It was fascinating for me. Harry made no demands on the horse at all, he just said, "Hey, I'm still over here if you want to come try to feel better," every so often with that gentle chap slap.

If you drive a horse forward around the pen, then back off that pressure, you create a vacuum that sucks the horse in. It's a trick that works, but the horse has very little choice in that scenario really because if the pressure applied is hard enough to drive him forward, then it is certainly hard enough for him to desire relief from it.

The conversation is something like, "Go this way because I say so...go...keep those feet moving...no, you can't stop yet, not yet...go some more...okay, there's an ear turning my way, he's getting tired of being pushed forward, bet he's ready to listen to me now...so stop and come here now!" Bingo, horse is hooked on, stops, and draws right up to you. But how does he feel about what just happened inside? Did he feel it was really a choice to stop and come to you? Just because now he follows you around wherever you go to keep from going out and running on the fence again, does that really mean he's emotionally settled with you and the situation? Will it carry over in a positive way to other parts of the relationship?

But, if like Harry in this example, you don't drive the horse in any way to begin with, then it is the horse who is choosing to go move around the fence at whatever speed and in whatever direction. You merely remind him that you are standing there by slapping your chap, without adding any additional direction.

In this situation, the conversation is more along the lines of, "Hey, you out there running circles because you're bothered inside, here I am...you might try coming and standing over here if you get tired of running circles out there. Feels pretty good standing here in the middle nice and easy. Whenever you want to give it a try, I'll just be right over here." The result is that the horse really decides when he comes to the human. The horse works it out for himself with only the slightest suggestion from the human. He is not driven in any way, but is moving his feet only because he chooses to, not because the human insists, or even suggests it.

I saw the difference then. I understood for the first time how much it means to the horse to be given as much time as it takes, not,

Harry riding at his place in Salome, Arizona. *(Tom Moates)*

just as much time as it takes as long as it doesn't take too long, after all this is a clinic.

This could take forty-five minutes, or shorter, or longer. The point is, I'd never before seen someone want to give that much time to letting a horse make a decision. In fact, I'd never seen anyone get in a round pen before without an agenda of how they were going to drive a horse's movements, however gently. And I think few realize how little choice the horse worked in a round-pen in the typical "natural horsemanshippy" way truly has. Whether it is because in a show type atmosphere or clinic the trainer senses the audience needs to see changes in the horse in five minutes for the wow factor, or a person just knows he can get results more quickly by intensifying the pressure and release. I had never before witnessed someone truly give a horse the time needed to work something like this out for himself. I began to see how the effect was more profound for the horse. He came to understand through his own doing how the difference in position and action feels, rather than being made to try this and that to be convinced one is better than the other.

This is just one example of many of equal gravity from my stay in Arizona. But, this case in point is particularly important because it provides the insight into what Sokeri told me when I returned home to Virginia.

I knew for quite awhile before my return that the first thing I'd do when I got back home was put Soke loose in the round pen and stand there and slap my chap with the end of the lead rope. I wasn't sure what she'd do. However, I knew that whatever she did would tell me who I had been two weeks earlier to her. I would be holding up a mirror to myself and having a look. That mare and I had spent time

Harry works one horse off another during Tom's trip to Arizona.
(Tom Moates)

nearly every day together for two years now, and that, coupled with days, weeks, and months of fairly decent pressure-and-release training, seemed to have our relationship going pretty well. So, I figured it might be a little confusing at first to have me act a little differently, but we'd see what she would do.

Within hours of getting home from the trip I was out in the round pen with her. I took up position in the center, which I'd done a million times before, then I gave my chap a half-way decent slap with the tail of the lead rope. I was shocked at her response. Sokeri took off and loped circles around the round pen. She trotted and loped for ten minutes, head up, thoughts as out of the corral as they could possibly have been. I just stood there realizing from the first ten seconds of this adventure that I was in the pen with a horse that didn't find any comfort being close to me. How odd! How completely wrong were my thoughts about how she had perceived me! How could I have missed so much?

I just stood there taking it in. Here was a horse that was not okay inside with the situation. She was both not seeking me for comfort, and lost because I had never before left her movements in the round pen completely up to her. I spend over an hour that day going through much the same thing I describe Harry doing above, except I never got her to settle down inside completely. She eventually did stand and relax a bit, and I stroked her nose and neck, but it would take several trips to the round pen over the next week to get her confirmed in the idea that standing still next to me in the middle of the pen felt better to her inside than being out on the fence moving around.

While this was fairly devastating for me to experience in a way, getting through it has brought about profound changes in our relationship. When I come to the pasture now, she often follows me along the fence until I enter and she can be with me. That never happened before. It seems it means so much to her that I finally got it. She'd been trying to tell me all along, so the side-affects have been interesting too. I no longer get a head tossing/shaking deal when I ask her to go from the walk to the trot, for example. It is bizarre to consider I may never have seen how Soke was twisted up inside, or that years more may have passed before I figured it out, if I ever figured it out. Which leads to the next question: so what am I still not seeing? You bet I'm trying to figure that out!

There are certainly increments of improvement we can make in our methods with horses if we genuinely seek to get better with them. There is no doubt that the type of pressure-and-release I used with Soke before the experience at Harry's was far better for her than what she had known previously in the mainstream horse world—I witnessed it before I bought her. But, I know the changes since Harry's have improved our relationship and her emotional response to my requests that much again, or perhaps even more.

The example presented here isn't made to say every horse should be worked this particular way in the round pen. It is NOT an exercise that is some silver bullet. It is just one small example of how one might rethink ways to improve things with a horse, and this one had particular meaning for Sokeri and me. The key is between the lines of this experience. It is to ask constantly, "How does my horse feel inside about things?"

Providing a horse real choices, along with all the time it takes for her to truly figure it out for herself, is the key that I mean to illustrate. Now, I try to carry that into all I do with horses.

Chapter 3

(Tom Moates)

Beginning Where We Want To End Up

The key to getting better with horses lies in the request.

The way we ask our horses for movement or stillness is the key to our relationship with them. The whole mountain of information on horsemanship that exists pretty much boils down to this basic fact, and all the various programs out there with their trade-marked ways ultimately iris down onto this one point. How a request is made of a horse is what differentiates all the styles one can apply to the art of working with horses.

As mentioned earlier, when I started exploring "natural horsemanship," what I first came across was the idea of "pressure and release." This idea was juxtaposed to "domination," "fear tactics," and the use of some devices that seemed pretty dark-agey which were commonly attributed to more mainstream training methods. The pressure and release idea was obviously more along the lines of what I was searching for, so I dove in.

The way I understood it then in my noviceness, long before I ever heard Harry speak about a horse's thought, was extremely mechanical. It amounted to, quite literally, poke the horse with something, like my thumb...if no reaction, dig it in deeper...still no reaction, poke the living daylights out of that horse until he moves away from the pain and irritation, and then release quickly. Build on that, and before long (hopefully for the horse's sake), you should have to poke far less, and eventually, not at all. A fingertip touch should do.

I haven't poked a horse in a long time now. I no longer need to poke a horse, not even a green one. Similarly, I don't look for a thin rope halter that pokes pressure points on a horse's face either, as some "natural" clinicians point out as a beneficial tool. I use rope halters quite a bit, but I use web halters just about as much. The thing is...I go about requesting movement from my horses in an entirely different way than what I learned early on. Through quite a bit of hands-on time with Harry, I began to see that many of those mechanical ideas never need to come into play if we begin somewhere else all together, and progress concentrating on working with a horse's thoughts rather than poking his hide.

One of the keys to this better way with horses is in the approach to how we make a request of a horse. Harry says it simply, "Begin where you want to end up." *opposite of Parelli*

The concept is incredibly easy to explain. Always, with complete consistency, begin asking a horse to do something in the way you eventually hope to see it in its refined state. That's it.

The difficulty isn't in understanding the idea, but in doing it.

A big problem is that we all realize the horse is never going to know what we're asking at first. Because of this little bit of knowledge all humans figure out pretty quickly, we have the tendency to automatically skip this first step. And likely the next couple as well. The result is that we typically start requesting a new movement from our horse in a way that produces results more quickly, but is therefore a much more severe cue than what we hope to require to get the job done further down the road.

For example, take the classic early scenario of wanting to ask a horse to move forward on the lead rope and begin to walk a circle around you. I like to raise my hand holding the lead rope up in front of me and to the side of the direction I want the horse to move in. In other words, if the horse is standing facing me and I want him to go counter clockwise around me, I'll take my left hand and hold the rope, lift it about as high as my left shoulder and lead the horse's thought out onto a circular line I want him to follow. I prefer to hold my hand out there the whole time I want the horse to walk around me, and I walk along with the horse in a small inner circle at the axis. But whatever you would like to be the ultimate ask to be for the horse to walk off around you, start there.

Even a very experienced horse person with a solid ability to project feel to a horse along the lead rope may get no response from the horse the first time he tries this deal. The horse has no past reference for it. So, even Harry may stand there with a horse just looking at him when he first begins this scenario. But it is critical to include this step. Without this step, even though the horse may not have a clue what it means, he has no choice to take it. Only when we offer the ultimate cue first do we provide the horse the opportunity to choose it. It must be there consistently, every time.

I recently spent a week with Harry in Virginia, and I made the joke to friends there that I had spent weeks over several years coming to clinics to watch Harry do nothing. The humor is in the irony. It is true, but by doing nothing Harry often gives horses a chance to break through with a right choice and get to feeling better about a situation in a way that makes a profound, positive, and permanent impression on them. The example here of circling is a good one to point this out. One might linger a little while there the first time or two, just offering up that initial ask for the horse to step off counter clockwise. This can be really counterintuitive to the demanding human who is not accustomed to waiting for much of anything these days. If you can get a nice, gentle, untroubled first step in the right direction...fantastic! Go rub that horse's neck and praise him! Then start over and build on that.

How many times have I seen horses driven to take that first step? Bunches. Whole bunches. The rope tail usually swings in the

Harry on Niji, the gelding clearly in a mental spot
where the clinician intended. *(Terry McCoy)*

human's opposite hand to amp up the pressure to drive the horse to take a step even before the hand to ask for the movement is in position. The horse is not offered the chance to make the choice first that way. At the very least, this kind of training starts with a hurried step. More often, it starts with a jolted, fleeing step. Folks find such snappiness quite appeasing, and often consider the quickness to be "respect" when really it is just a troubled horse. That kind of motion and emotional conditioning is getting built in there from the very first moments if you drive the horse into taking a step. That is exactly what I built into Sokeri that exploded to the surface in the round pen when I got back from Arizona as described in the previous chapter.

If you linger there doing nothing more than offering the ask to step off with the lead rope for five minutes--all the blood leaving your hand until it is about to fall off--you may get the sweetest, calmest first step in the world. Build on that, and you may discover you just saved yourself months of working trouble out of the horse which inadvertently might be built into him in the form of flight or resentment caused by driving him more quickly to that first step. It is even possible you have avoided putting something negative in there that might never leave the horse. Plus, if you drive the horse into something initially, he never feels like he really had a choice or came to the conclusion on his own. These little things are huge to the horse, and so many people just never begin to comprehend or consider them.

Now, if the horse just isn't getting it, Harry will slap his chap with a hand or the tail of the halter rope. This is not to drive the horse. This is merely to break the mental status quo. He is saying to the horse, "standing there isn't going to work out feller...start searching for what my hand holding the rope this way means."

Note that this is completely different from swinging the tail of a rope in behind the withers and whacking the horse to drive him in the opposite direction to step away from pressure.

Harry may need to whack his chaps several times, but eventually that horse will free up mentally and try moving in the right direction. A really stuck horse may need encouragement after only beginning to take his thought slightly to the side. That's often called the "slightest try," and deserves recognition to help build confidence towards the further goal. Other times, a horse picks up the feel Harry is putting out there, and a little chap slap is all that is needed to break the feet loose and have the horse moving nicely.

If the feel in this example is always the first part of the request each time the deal is started, then it is present in the succession of events that get a result. That bit of feel must be present each time so it eventually can be intuited by the horse. The truth is, most likely the horse recognizes that feel from the very first time, he just doesn't have a frame of reference for what it means. If the handler is consistent in including it and how it is presented each time, the horse will soon get the association between it and taking a step.

If the seemingly ridiculously light first "ask" is skipped, however, as just an impractical waste of time at the early stage, the horse is done a disservice. If we really want to present a horse choices, then we have to actually do our part and take the time it takes to make the effort to present real choices every step of the way, every time we do new things with our horses.

Another part of this deal that I always find challenging is just to have the focus to begin where I want to end up. Unconsciously, I find it easy to slip into the moment of working with the horse. This

Tom works with Jubal. *(Carol Moates)*

zone is great sometimes. The world melts away except for me and my equine companion, and I'm completely absorbed in the progress and interaction of the moment. While this is typically a good thing, I find it also can add to the trouble of forgetting first steps.

Say, returning to the above example for instance, I remember to start by putting a little feel first on the line, then go to smacking my chaps to get that horse focused and he takes that first step. "Alright," I think, "I'm getting somewhere." This gets repeated the same way three times with similar results since the horse is pretty mentally stuck, but on the fourth go-round I forget the feel that seems not to be working anyway and just slap the chap. "Awesome!" I think, all together forgetting where I want to end up. Then, I'm so excited about the progress being made in the circling deal that I just start seeing how light a slap I can use to get a step, but forget all about the feel first deal. I'm just so focused and intent on the progress of circling that I simply forget to keep track of the overarching goal—to consistently begin where I want to end up so that I can eventually, actually get there. I'm teaching the horse to move off a slap at this point, not the feel on the rope I ultimately seek to have there.

Yet another trap I fall into is one of simple busy-ness. I spend plenty of time in the round pen with horses, but that isn't my goal. Now, while I know with certainty the round pen and arena are very useful tools towards training horses, there is no doubt a great many humans choose to never leave them. I spend time working in them so the horse and I can leave the confines of the small space behind and go out into the world for work and play. I seek to use these incredible creatures for real stuff. Trail riding, checking fences, helping check on cattle, and generally making a nuisance of myself is the real goal for me.

What I find is that when I push the envelope and head out of the controlled environment of the practice corral, often many things occur at once. I may have wind blowing tall weeds around me, squirrels jumping in leaves, and other horses in earshot calling out. In an instant, there may be reins to keep straight in my hands, a rope to avoid getting tangled up in, a vehicle roaring down the road, another horse needing attention, a heifer with an issue that needs looking into disappearing into the sunset, and the horse under my butt beginning to lose it. It is in these moments that I definitely lose track of "starting where I want to end up" with my requests of my horse. And it's a real shame too, because if I could keep it together and stay light in that real world situation, it would redouble the horse's confidence in me and more deeply instill the refined requests I seek in that horse.

What usually happens though, is that my reflexes, inexperience, and information overload end up with me jerking on the reins and generally sending crazy mixed up signals to the horse—not the most productive means of building confidence.

My mare, Sokeri, is such a challenging horse. I have worked constantly with her for several years now, and she provides a never ending flow of subjects for my writing on getting better with horses. Many of the problems I face with her today, I've worked on in many ways since the beginning of our relationship. Sometimes there even seems to be progress frustratingly followed by regression, without any apparent reason for it from my human perspective.

Recently I asked Harry about this. "Do you think," I started, pausing to try and phrase the question just right, "that there are horses, like Soke, that just never can get over certain issues no matter what we do? Or, do you think it is always in how the human approaches them? In other words, am I just not able to present things right for her, and support her in the way she needs to get past some of these things? Or, is she hardwired for it, and I'll never get there with her?"

"I've wondered about that myself many times," Harry replied. "And the more I see, the more I'm convinced that the problem is in how we approach the horse."

Harry has seen thousands of horse problems arise and disappear, and short of physical pain (an injury or ill fitting saddle for instance), he feels strongly that the key to getting problems resolved with our horses is in how we make our requests of them.

A horse can move for a human for various motivations. The inspiration we hopefully seek is that the horse moves because he wants to. It is understood that horses also move to flee from pain or fear. They will move to go through the motions with humans, to just try and get by but withdraw mentally and be shut down. There is a difference between a horse just trying to survive, doing all it can to just get by, and a horse engaged in his work and play, eager and interested to go with the guidance of a human.

Even a horse that doesn't misbehave and gets all the movements right may be less than willing. My mare Sokeri is great at tricking me into thinking we're in the groove and she's having a great ride following the lightest cue—seemingly reading my mind at times—and then just go off in her own direction, mentally and physically. I'm left wondering, "was it that big scary chickadee that just flew by, or that car horn across the river two miles away?" The bottom line that I have to face with her is: she only trusts me so far. She is quick to take back the control she volunteers willingly sometimes if push comes to shove.

The idea of pressure and release is the basis for working with horses in what I have sometimes called the Better Way. But, as I was discussing earlier about the poking deal, there are many ways this can be implemented with varying results. Natural horsemanshippy or not, use of pressure and release can create the situation where a horse is motivated to move away from pressure and/or pain, which is not the same as moving willingly. Yet, to really confuse things, it is essentially pressure and release that gets things started on the road towards that willing movement in a horse.

One of the greatest contributions Harry makes to horses is getting humans to ask themselves, "How does this horse feel about things inside?" This one question is in itself an approach. If we start with this thought foremost in our minds, then our next step is more likely going to be with the horse's true needs in mind. This is not an A, B, C proposition—it is not a how-to with nice clean steps that work for every horse each time. It is more of a way of thinking which allows us to best use whatever we have in our horsemanship repertoire to our horse's greatest advantage. It may even produce in us the desire and ability to use our imaginations to invent new ways to reach a particular horse.

The application of pressure and release should always be to show a horse ways to feel better inside. The horse with a problem is likely showing a sign of not feeling right emotionally about his situation. If you are in a round pen with your horse and he is spazzing out, he's not okay with the situation and isn't looking to you for comfort, but is rather seeking other ways to find it (moving his feet, looking for a way out of the corral, or calling for other herd mates for instance). It is your job to show him it doesn't have to be that way. Your job and responsibility to your horse is to guide him to see that he will feel better inside when he makes the choice you suggest—one that you set up for him and comforts him when he gets it worked out, and he will think was his choosing. Consistency reinforces this and makes it solid

Consistently beginning where he wanted to end up,
Harry gets a horse bowing to a cue. *(Tom Moates)*

and dependable to the horse.

Starting where you want to end up is a huge part of getting a horse feeling better inside, regardless of what movements you're asking for. It does so because it gives him the choice of getting to that refined place from the start, it focuses us on keeping our handling consistent, and it also focuses our minds on thinking about where we want to get with the request—to a light, willing, happy, and responsive partner. Expect that it will happen, go about it like it will happen, and then don't be surprised when it happens!

Chapter 4

(Tom Moates)

The Myth Of Natural Horsemanship

Before going further, I'm compelled to clear the air regarding the term, "natural horsemanship" for my own peace of mind. Especially since it is pretty much unavoidable given the subject of this book.

I must inform you that natural horsemanship is a myth—it

does not actually exist. I know that sounds odd coming from the author of a book and countless articles on the subject. So, let me explain what I mean, and shed some light onto the true nature of those two words strung together before I tackle anything else.

Natural horsemanship is a term that casts such a wide net that it means, at most, very little, and very likely nothing at all. It apparently came into usage when the clinician, Pat Parelli, coined it to try and describe what he was doing with his horsemanship program, and later wrote a book by the same name. The public, which always seeks to categorize people, places, things, and everything else under headings to try and make it all conform to some sense of law and order, scooped it up and lumped a huge spectrum of stuff under it.

On the other hand, it hasn't hurt a whole slew of clinicians and practitioners of every sort to have some umbrella under which to tell the public that what they are doing is new, different, correct, valuable, and basically an innovative deal—whether that was actually the case or not. The "natural" association in the name easily aligns itself with increasingly popular environmentalist ideas, so it grabs the attention and quick endorsement of a growing and financially secure group of people already recycling, driving hybrids, and buying earth friendly dish soap. It is without question the spearhead of a marketing coup with a great many millions of dollars spent to its credit annually. It was so successful that it swiftly and firmly became established in the global marketplace as well.

It reminds me of the term "organic." Some years ago, a few folks coined that phrase to mean that the food they produced was free from pesticides, chemical fertilizers, and other potentially hazardous ingredients. Today, largely due to the fact that organics became such

Tom working hard in Arizona. *(Michéle Jedlicka)*

a desirable marketable item fetching high prices and developing wide consumer confidence, the term has been hijacked by big business. These days, thanks it seems to the lobbying efforts of corporations, one may even legally label food "organic" that includes some non-organic ingredients, which is no where close to the original usage. As a descriptive term, it is so diluted now that in fact food must be labeled "100% organic" to actually mean what used to be (and is probably now mis-understood by the buying masses today as) "organic."

Or, take the term "free." I remember when something was free, it meant there was no cost for it. These days, I've got 2100 free minutes on my cell phone that cost me $120 a month. That's just not the true meaning of free...but here we find ourselves and our language altered by marketing and new usage. So what do we do now? Do we need to say 100% free to mean free?

Back to natural horsemanship. It is just such a mis-nomer. First of all, there are numerous clinicians that I know that do not call themselves natural horsemen, and loath the term being used to describe them. However, they get lumped under the heading anyway by their pupils, authors, journalists, and public at-large that externally force the label upon them. Shouldn't they know best what they are and what they do? Then there are also many clinicians that go out of their way to make certain they are associated with natural horsemanship.

"Horse whisperer" is another interesting and very closely related example. Because of the wide audience of the Hollywood film by that name, non-horse people in particular like to apply the term to many horse folk that also are lumped under the natural horsemanship heading. However, to a much larger extent, horse whisperer for some reason developed a somewhat negative connotation among horse folk.

It seems generally politically incorrect to use it in horse circles, and one who does use it to describe himself instantly denotes himself as an outsider, even to many natural horsemanship enthusiasts. Perhaps it has to do with one of my all-time favorite clinician quotes from Buck Brannaman, who said something like, "If someone comes up to you and calls himself a horse whisperer, put your hand on your wallet and get away as quickly as you can!" It seems that the general meaning has shifted now, and one who calls himself a horse whisperer is thought to be an obvious fraud.

Then there is the question of the term itself. Just what whispering is actually a part of horse whispering? Maybe some, maybe none. Who knows? It's all very quiet and mysterious.

Natural horsemanship as a compound phrase suffers terribly from this problem. It clearly seeks to describe subjects in the realm of horsemanship, but what is natural about it? I've heard clinicians that didn't like being lumped under the heading argue to distance themselves from it things like, "If you put a halter or saddle on a horse, there's nothing natural about that, is it?" Good point.

There's another one as well. Many people think the most completely "natural" horses in the world are the mustangs of the American west, but they aren't the least bit natural either. The best book I ever read on that subject is Paula Morin's compilation of 63 interviews with all kinds of people that have extensive personal experience with the wild horses of the Great Basin titled, *Honest Horses* (University of Nevada Press, 2006). She makes an outstanding point that is true but few people seem to realize:

Only the plain and stocky Przewalski'a Horse of Mongolia fits the scientifically rigorous definition for a bona fide wild horse.... Regardless of how many generations horses have lived on the range [the American west], feral is the accurate description for them. They are domestic animals that have returned to live in a wild state.

Harry makes a point at a clinic on Jubal. *(Tom Moates)*

And the fact that horses were re-introduced to North America by the Spanish only a few hundred years ago after a millennia long disappearance from this continent puts them at odds with the natural eco-system here. It is a relationship thus wrought with difficulties as the horses' grazing habits destroy the natural balance of the ranges where they populate the regions. They are like Kudzu, or Starlings, or any other foreign and therefore un-natural visitor to this country that has profound, lopsided, and potentially devastating affects on the truly natural and native species here.

So, if mustangs in the wild, almost universally considered the most natural of all natural horses by the masses, aren't natural, then what in the world possibly can be natural about any modern human horse interaction? Especially those that involve man made tack, fencing, and tools like flags or crops?

The "natural" derives from Parelli's initial usage of the term, and in particular in his book, *Natural Horse*Man*Ship*. His reason for coining the phrase, he states in that narrative, had to do with describing the method of communicating he was working on between human and horse. He believed his games and pressure-and-release methods were, as he says: "native, instinctive, inborn, inherent, and intuitive." Now therein lies an interesting use of natural. The term natural horsemanship is basically meant to be synonymous with something along the lines of, natural communication with horses, or speak Horse, or interact with horses the way they interact with each other in a herd and get more done with them more gently than most other humans do. That I can begin to follow, but in practice now there are such variations out there that still it hardly nails down anything specific. Is Californios style vaquero traditional horsemanship natural horsemanship, for instance? What about someone who trains with a natural horsemanship program and then goes and competes with that horse...can that still be considered natural horsemanship in the incredibly unnatural show ring? You get the idea.

Another mis-conception that runs rampant, and is eagerly proclaimed by some, is that natural horsemanship is brand new.

First of all, as I said at the top, natural horsemanship doesn't exist.... What is it? Seven games? Switching to a rope halter? Riding a Wade saddle? Pressure and release? Using a round pen? Using a flag? It is indefinable because it isn't static. There is a lack of concrete rules that define natural horsemanship. Working in the most beneficial way with horses possible (if that pitiful turn of phrase puts us somewhere in the realm of natural horsemanship) is a moving target. No two horses are the same. Any one specific method will have incredibly different results between different individuals. Presenting it as A THING that can be understood, defined, and taught, is just wrong. It is, if anything, an overarching kind of approach under which can fall whole ranges of methods, and even some rather harsh ones might be natural horsemanship by some standards if used by the right person at the right time on the right horse.

Second of all, the idea that many of the methods commonly boxed and sold to the public as innovations created recently by some clinicians comprising a totally new revolution in working with horses is likewise misleading. Really exceptional horse folk have existed at times since humans began working with horses. The main difference today is that the discussion about how one gets that good is at an entirely new level. It is a global discussion, and the language of horsemanship is morphing to meet this challenge. But many examples exist to show

how the ideas so often now packaged and sold as original breakthroughs have been around for ages.

I was recently watching a PBS documentary on the incredible English upper class woman turned Montana pioneer, Evelyn Cameron, when suddenly they mentioned a quote from one of her diary entries that I recognized instantly as what today we would call "desensitizing" a horse. I looked it up. She wrote exactly this on March 26, 1895 (the grammar is forgone a bit in this entry, but the meaning is clear):

> Took the foals down to water. They were frightened of the clothes on the washing line blowing in the wind, therefore I made them go round & round the length of the line. Little grey [foal] was awfully willfully threw itself down & skinned my fingers so I tied them up, put gloves on & broke one at a time. Had hard battle with Figs (iron grey) to get her to go under the line, but got both finally so that they let the clothes flap all round them.

Ultimately, what natural horsemanship is if anything, is a shift in the language of horsemanship. How people change the language of horsemanship at large and share ideas as an attempt to impart ways of improving the horse/human relationship is where some consistency may be found under this heading. But, the frequent application of the term "natural horsemanship" to all kinds of people and methods muddies the waters.

It might be best for those of us seeking a better way to get better with horses to narrow our focus to a clearer understanding of what individuals are really doing with horses. Specifics are truly telling, and it's perhaps best to leave the enormously broad über-headings out of the arena.

I just really needed to say all that once and for all. So back to other stuff.

Chapter 5

(Carol Moates)

Trotting Circles

Sokeri and I were managing to log quite a bit of saddle time at this point of our relationship. About six months had passed since my return from visiting Harry in Arizona. The rides were good. Tacking was going smoothly. I mounted these days from the ground, fence, or tailgate without issues. And, while we as a team still no-doubt lacked finesse, we had traveled miles of fences together checking for trouble, and gotten through quite a few obstacles in this mountainous farm land of the Blue Ridge without wrecks or major hassles.

I even convinced my mare to willingly step up onto a big stone flight of steps at the front of our house, a feat obviously way more exciting to me than my wife, Carol, who told me so, (something about horses not belonging on porches...I forget exactly how she put it). Since then, I've decided stepping up onto stumps in the woods is an all around better idea, and we even had this trick down to a fine art by this point.

Getting from the seriously awkward situation of being a rank beginner, to that of a horseman who can at least begin to work through some problems on his own, was where I found myself then. A kind of horsemanship adolescence. I might call it: being just a tiny bit beyond "knowing just enough to be completely dangerous" when trying to get better with horses. Or, being at that point where I can keep track of more than just one single thing at a time when riding. Or, better yet, at the point where I can reach into the horsemanship toolbox, pull out some bit of learned information, commingle it with some experience, and actually work through a problem with my horse in an original way once in awhile.

On this particular day, I saddled Soke for a ride in the afternoon. It was a fairly decent fall day. I never need a reason to ride. I love to just saddle up and see where we get to in our relationship on any given day. It seems, however, to help us both when I do have some kind of purpose in mind when we set out. The night before, we had endured 4 inches of rain and stiff winds, so I figured we had better check on a few fences as we traveled, so I had a focus in mind.

The tailgate was down on the truck, so I hopped up there. She came along beside it, and I slid easily over into the saddle. Once settled in, with my feet in the stirrups, I picked up the reins and initiated stepping off at a walk.

I planned on staying at an energetic walk; she had other plans and began to trot.

A day earlier, a seed had been planted in my brain which sprouted at that instant. I'd done a really decent job of pestering Harry in the previous year, and there were more times than I could count by then where his teaching got through to me. Even now it happens, both on the spot in his presence and on time-delay where something he said or did pops into my head at just the right moment much later.

This particular time was no exception, although his words came to me in an unusual way, via the internet. I was looking on his website (www.harrywhitney.com) to check on some writing of mine getting posted there, when I came across a clinic report from 2001 by Beth Anne Doblado. It drew my attention for some unknown reason. I opened it and my eyes scrolled right on down to one particular quote she had of Harry's: "When riding, at any step you should be able to ask the hind end to step under and front end to step over and walk out in a circle, all 4 feet moving equally."

At the time, I registered the idea simply wondering if I could do it. Now, on Soke, with me walking in the saddle and her trotting beneath it, the idea of just going into a circle came to mind initiated from the memory of that quote. I steered her to the right....

As I said earlier, I've gotten beyond the point where I can only keep one single thing at a time straight in my head when riding a horse.

Sokeri and Tom riding at home in Virginia. *(Rainey Houston)*

This is one of those multi-tasking instances. About nine thoughts were going at once in my head, and really the whole deal just happened as a real knee-jerk reflex, instantaneously. The nine thoughts went like this (try to read them all at once while riding for the proper effect):

--the little booger is taking off on her own,
--does she do this much,
--well, actually yes, idiot, she does,
--right, true...usually I haul back on the reins and block her forward motion forcing her to slow down, don't I,
--guess that must not really work too well since I'm looking for a walk still, three years later, and she's still trotting,
--hey, I read that thing Harry said last night, let's just try to turn and circle,
--you think trotting a tight circle will throw you off and leave you a crumpled heap on the ground,
--I doubt it, I'm hanging in this saddle no matter what,
--hey, guess what...if we go into a circle every time she trots when I want us to walk, maybe....

Before I got that last one fully formed, she was tired of trotting that little circle I'd sent us into, and came down to a walk.

I released the turn and let her go straight.

She walked about five strides then broke into that trot again.

I bent her over into a circle, to the left this time, kept her there for about one and a half revolutions, at which point she brought herself back to a walk and I let us move on straight at that exact instant.

We went through the same walk-a-few-strides-then-go-to-trotting thing again. Then, on the forth trotting circle trip, she was getting upset. As we went into the circle she threw her head around, then lowered it, and I could feel in her body we were really close to going to the rodeo. I could tell she was aggravated about these circles which were messing with her plans, but before expending the effort it takes to buck, she tried slowing to the walk. Voila, she got to go straight.

That seemed to be the point at which everything changed. She quite suddenly settled into the rhythm of the walk I was looking for, and seemed content about it. Harry is always asking, "How does the horse feel about what is going on?" When she was wanting to break into a trot, perhaps she was searching for a way to alleviate some worry going on inside of her. It seems she was not completely okay with our situation, and was seeking to trot away from it to find a better feeling spot in herself.

All the years of our work together, and I still could not just slip onto my horse and walk without her expressing this trouble inside her. Her determination to trot wasn't bad enough that I couldn't make her straighten up and fly right at the walk if I wanted to—that is what I had been doing. But, that obviously never solved the problem. Now, quite suddenly, I had a horse that felt very different as we walked on. And this was only ten minutes into the ride.

The difference in this new approach I took, looking at it closely after the fact, I realize is based in what I had gleaned from Harry's teaching in several instances. It has to do with truly giving a horse choices. Before, when I insisted Soke walk, not trot, by hauling back on the reins, I was forcing the issue. Even by timing releases on the reins perfectly to the desired transition, this particular horse

→ If she had been really bothered, the bit would not have stopped her.

felt no choice in the matter. She was bothered and let me know it by wanting to move her feet faster. By blocking those feet with the bit, sometimes even stopping her completely, and even backing her up at times, I was taking a bothered horse wanting to flee and doing the worst thing possible—blocking her feet, and trapping her in a slow pace or a stop. She could not diffuse her anxiety because in her mind ("from the horse's point of view," as Harry says), she had no choice in the matter, and I, the evil wrongdoer who just didn't appreciate her opinion, was trapping her in this miserable situation.

In the new trotting circles situation, I realized we could have a conversation about this wanting to take off deal in a completely different way. The circles were my input. The beauty of this new deal was that I in no way blocked her forward motion. When turning her, I was very careful to use only the absolute minimum pressure necessary for the turn, keeping as slack a rein as possible. I in no way regulated her speed, which remained completely her choice. I only steered our direction.

It seemed to me now that Sokeri had never really cared where we were headed anyway. Moving her feet fast, wherever we went, was her deal. In this new situation, she could trot all she wanted to, it just had to be in a circle. Apparently, trotting a circle isn't really all that great for the horse because it took very few of them for her to decide she'd rather walk. I was never sure this would work out right; indeed it was so spur-of-the-moment, there was no time for pre-conceived notions at all. But, when it worked out the right way so quickly, I became consistent in my role of insisting trot/circle or walk/straight line, so she clearly saw these new options as the rule. The difference from the previous way I dealt with it, was that to her, I was presenting her with real options.

The rest of the ride went on for about an hour and a half (complete with stepping her front feet onto stumps, not steps, for fun). In that entire time, I circled her for choosing to trot away from me again only twice, and with quick positive results and no resentment. It was truly awesome.

There are only a very few instances where I remember a conversation with a horse going so quickly for me. I'm not going to tell you I'm convinced this will work in any situation, with any horse, or that it will even work with Sokeri always in the future, even though it has at this point made a profound change. The important aspect of this example is in that underlying general approach which I have picked up from being around Harry: asking, "How does a horse feel about things?" If we start there when addressing any horse problem, then we are at the beginning of seeing how to truly make things better for a horse, and thereby not "correct" a problem, but dissolve it all together.

I finally saw my mare's need to move her feet as essential to her inner emotional well being. I could block that till the end of time with those reins and she would never feel better about it, even if I got the walk I was looking for. But, since I'm not looking for a walk, but rather looking for a horse happy to walk along with me, that first answer wasn't an answer at all.

Only by presenting her with real choices, and letting her know she can choose to move her feet however she needs to, can get her okay with that. It is presenting things in a way that she decides about them on some level that works for her. She needed to say to herself, "Well, guess I'll walk, since there's no need to expend all this energy trotting in a circle," instead of, "Oh no...danger, fear, strong opinion, whatever...must trot, must trot, stop blocking me by pulling on my mouth...must trot, get that bit out of the way!" With Soke, only when she had that choice available finally, did she come to a better place inside herself. Then, the walk seemed like no-big-deal. The underlying basis for her change truly seemed to be just that simple.

The phrase, "make the right thing easy and the wrong thing hard" gets tossed around quite a bit at clinics. I always wince when I hear the second part of that because I think humans are really quick to gloss over the "easy" part and go right to the "making the wrong thing hard" part. We are really good at that, and the extreme version of it is called punishment, which has no place in horse/human relationships. But, the example here fits that full statement, but in a particular way.

The right thing easy is simply release for doing what I wanted in the first place, a straight brisk walk. The wrong thing hard is the more difficult, dreaded trotted circle. But here, notice that the wrong thing hard is actually far better for Soke than that other alternative I was giving her—blocking forward motion, period.

Obviously I can't have my horse just calling the shots all over the place, so I can't let her just choose whatever speed she wants whenever, especially if it intensifies her fear and flight instincts. It must be changed. But, like with a horse in a round pen, here we worked through something while those feet were moving so she got to a place where she no longer needed to trot.

I'm happy to meet her half way and get to a nice walk by trotting a few circles. When I stopped blocking her feet and let her make the choice about them, even though I substituted circles for stops, the consistency in the approach let her know that at any time she felt the need to trot, she is perfectly welcomed to...in a circle.

The clincher here, I believe, is that Sokeri knows she has the option open to her to trot anytime now, and I won't stop her—that was simply not the case before. Before, I kept telling her, "no...absolutely not," which is quite different from, "fine, trot, we'll just go over here and do it till you're finished." Suddenly, it diffused that anxiety in her. Just having the choice meant that much to her, which has meant every bit as much to me too.

Chapter 6

Pushing The Envelope

"In our comfort, there's no room for growth," I heard Harry say. The reference was to working with horses. Harry's horsemanship clinics usually are limited to six riders and typically run over the span of a week. The result of this arrangement is that these intimate groups enjoy ample opportunity to probe deeply into their horsemanship abilities and inabilities (and Harry's brain) if they have the courage and interest to go there. The above comment came during a regular round table discussion that immediately followed breakfast. The group rehashed the previous day's events, which turned to one fellow's somewhat timid feelings about firming up with his horse to find improvement in their relationship.

As is so often the case, what our horses confront us with has much wider reaching applications in life. "In our comfort, there's no room for growth," I replayed in my head. My focus slipped suddenly to several personal flashbacks. Stepping into a round pen for the first time to work with a horse came to mind, as did the first time I managed to get a horse to canter. And then there was the first time getting into the saddle....

Each of these moments signified a huge leap from the safety of a sedentary existence in my routine life. An outright jump over the cliff at the edge of the known world into the abyss beyond my knowledge and experience. A tightrope walk without a net. A canter without a bridle. An act of faith that somewhere in that uncharted wilderness "out there" was a way through uniquely mine to somewhere new. That, quite frankly, while there was nothing to ensure I wouldn't be wrecked, injured, or killed, I needed to push out of the stagnating areas of my life and into a realm of new possibilities. Otherwise, I'd begin to suffer consequences from the lack of action, like never getting to the point of riding a horse in the first place.

Surviving each of these monumental equestrian moments, and so many others as well, taught me much about the world and about myself. I won't lie and say there weren't wrecks, because there were some real doozies. But, in retrospect, these deviations from the comfortable--with all their worry, angst, and bruises (oh yeah, and those broken ribs when I came off at a canter that time)--instigated profoundly positive changes in my horsemanship, but in my development as a person as well.

I wondered if this would be the case for this fellow at Harry's clinic facing a new day in the round pen with his horse. New confidence only comes from diving over the line out of the comfort zone and into some other place where new knowledge awaits us. Once on the other side, however, we see it's not really an abyss out there waiting to swallow us up like some savage beast--we just couldn't see what was there from our former vantage point. That new experience and knowledge then becomes part of our working repertory. Nowhere is this more true than with horses. If we want to see a change in them, we must change something in our approach. Changing ourselves to get a new approach that works with a horse...well, that's the tough part.

The great thing about a trustworthy teacher who already has visited the nether-world of horsemanship and returned (that place still invisible to us poor pupils), is that he can guide us and help us prepare for what comes next. Still, it is we who first-hand must enter the round pen and face the fire breathing dragon (or very sweet mare, as the case may be). Finding faith within ourselves to step in new directions, especially when it is quite challenging, ultimately helps us build confidence. Confidence in life is a good thing, and it is exceptionally positive to have with horses.

Horses are a confidence barometer. In general, they relax when a strong, sure being is present. Confidence is contagious with them. Likewise, uncertainty in a human working with a horse breeds dubious

Bruce Lawson getting on well with Wrangler at the clinic he hosted
in Virginia. *(Terry McCoy)*

results at best from the highly sensitive equine.

My thoughts drifted back to the ongoing discussion around the table, which soon wrapped up. Before long, we headed outside to the round pen, and this fellow took a turn with the mare. Being very kind hearted, it was easy to see he longed to nurture a bond with this horse by approaching her nice and easy in every motion and every gesture he made. Great care was taken to do nothing spooky or harsh. Likewise, it was easy for the observer with some experience to see the mare searching for clarity in just what was being asked of her. She was clearly willing to do something (perhaps anything), but simply not finding it in his requests. She was unable to feel confident about what she was supposed to do, so she half-heartedly did a little bit of whatever she could think of.

He grappled with the situation. I sat there wincing behind the brim of my straw hat—partly from being in-the-know about his wimpy body position and don't-rock-the-boat gentleness, and partly because I had been through the very same thing some years earlier, so I knew how he felt.

This new day in the round pen, however, he understood the problems he faced with the horse differently. That morning's feedback from Harry and the other observers provided new insights for him. The battle I now witnessed really was within himself. He sought to find assertiveness even though he was quite worried that firming up with a horse was a recipe for driving her away, possibly for good, rather than getting her close and willing with him.

At this point the mare was constantly just leaving the scene mentally and floundering about unguided. Clearly not what a rider wants with a mount, and seeing this on the ground only meant it spilled over when they saddled up. The situation required he firm up with her so she would react in a more trusting way to his requests. Part of this simply has to do with clarity. Wishy washy, pretty please requests often appear very convoluted to the horse, and human onlookers as well.

To firm up, we often are faced with a more precise need to know exactly what we are asking the horse to do. It can happen that suddenly we realize that, well, we really aren't exactly sure what we want the horse to do. If we ask the horse to back, but have no clue ourselves how many steps, or where we would like the horse to end up, how is the horse ever going to know for sure what we want? The horse can't possibly know that if we don't know it ourselves.

The other part has to do with the horse's belief that we are serious. If the horse doesn't find us dependable, trustworthy, assertive, or consistent then the confidence they need to follow and trust in is simply not going to be there.

It seemed to me I could sense this inner turmoil boiling inside the fellow from my seat thirty feet away. It was a personal threshold for this young man. Getting bigger with that horse ran counter to his very pacifistic demeanor. But then he did it.

It may not have looked big to a spectator. It really was just a larger body posture and some assertive energy on the lead rope. But for that guy, it was a huge step. And for that horse, used to him and unaccustomed to that, likewise it was huge. She reacted a bit shocked at first, but quickly fell in to the moves he now clearly asked for.

It really isn't important to explain exactly what he was asking for at that moment—that doesn't matter, because this isn't about trying to create some series of steps for everyone to follow. This is about one problem many of us have, and how I saw someone find the courage to get better with a horse with the help of a skilled teacher. This is about finding that courage and pushing the envelope of our comfort zone so we can grow.

Later when I asked Harry about this episode, he articulated

Things get a little spunky between Tom and Niji. *(Terry McCoy)*

my feelings about what I had seen very well. Harry said: "He lacked confidence because he lacked faith in the outcome. Then, when he had faith that the outcome would be better, his confidence grew. He just had to go through that uncomfortable phase."

That's what it is: pushing the envelope of our experience is "that uncomfortable phase."

Chapter 7

Hurrying

"What 'cha hurrying for?" Harry Whitney asked.

Feet propped up on a block of wood, the clinician sat reclined in a chair but didn't miss a thing, gazing intently through the metal fence panels at the action in the round pen. One sensed his calm and certain willingness in that particular moment: unflustered...unhurried... universally understanding the situation before him.

One also instantly realized the wisdom in the question he blurted out. It was simultaneously question and answer. I, for one, was dumbfounded. Immediately I stopped focusing so hard on what might be the specifics of the issues going on inside the round corral— some A, B, C answer to trouble or mis-behavior (How is the flag held? What's the expression on the person's face? Did that gelding trot before asked?), and smiled when I realized the woman was rushing the horse in everything she asked of him. That hyped-up mindset had tainted all that had unfolded with the horse to that point. She emitted a frazzle of hurried energy, and with it came a frazzled horse.

Sometimes it takes a master who is beyond the murky territory of trying so hard to get it right, or a child so innocent that the obvious is still beautifully obvious, to point out the most observable things, I thought then. I made a mental note of it.

If you leave one of Harry's clinics with nothing else, you likely will depart with a new found appreciation for asking the question when around a horse: "How does this horse feel about things just now?" followed close behind by, "How can I improve things for this horse?"

If we had asked the horse in front of us then how he felt at that moment, "rushed, dang it!" would have rolled off the tip of his tongue, no doubt. But, just an instant before Harry dropped his question bomb, I was certain what I saw in the head shaking, taut body, and less-than-smooth transitions was some mental resistance to the person's requests in the round pen. While I was sort-of right in my analysis, it wasn't resistance to those particular cues per-se that I saw, but rather an outward sign of dissatisfaction to how the requests were presented.

As a spectator, I looked far too hard for answers. My focus narrowed and missed the simple intensity of overarching hurry in the person in general. I saw only the physical cues she sent out and the horse's reactions. I perceived only the nuts-and-bolt of this and that.... How amazingly simple of Harry to sum up so much in a quick, "What 'cha hurrying for?" And how stupid I felt not to see that forest for the trees!

There are, in literal truth, really no trees to be seen in the immense vastness of the Arizona desert at Harry's place in Salome where this unfolded. It's the kind of place that exudes a timelessness. Traveling to there from wherever folks' homes are, leaving behind their schedules and pressing matters, trailering in a horse, and having a week or two to devote to an intimate clinic with Harry, one would expect it to be clearly established in the mind of a person that there is nowhere to rush to. No job, no dentist appointment, nor news show on TV to busy our schedules and compete for our waking hours. Yet, I remarked in my journal from that time how Harry repeatedly made the point to various clinic goers not to rush, rush, rush things with a horse.

Each time Harry made the point, it specifically referred to how someone sent his or her horse around the round pen. I came to the conclusion that many people (I include myself in this group, thus my point of writing it down at the time for future reference) just naturally have the tendency to hasten what they do with horses when working with them. Whether on lead or at liberty, folks sent their horses around at a hundred miles an hour. Then when Harry asked, "What 'cha hurrying for?" they'd stop, think for a minute, but never have an actual answer to the question. They seemed to be surprised and puzzled by it at first, but almost as quickly recognized that regardless of the "why," it is the rush they had in themselves spilling over into the work with their horses that was the root of some of their trouble. Resolving this overarching hurriedness was Harry's point in asking the question.

I think the real answer is clearly that it is simply how we humans tend to operate in this culture. We don't have to speed in our vehicles--no one insists that we do, it burns more fuel, and it is illegal, but we do it all the time anyway. We rush all over the place each day like it is somehow going to help us get more accomplishments squashed into those precious few hours we are blessed to have. What it achieves, really, is to hurt the quality of focus we provide to whatever tasks we undertake. It is no big secret that mistakes, shoddy work, and even injuries come from being too hurried. And, after we blast around for hours, or days, spiraling in our various chosen directions like maniacs, we get into a round pen with our horses. It's no great wonder we get in there and rush them too, unaware. After all, that's normal isn't it?

Harry was fantastic during my two week stay in Arizona at showing there is no need for all that buzzing about with your horse. You can calmly ask him for a walk. You can just as quietly ask for a direction change. In fact, you can even ask for the exciting speed of a trot or canter with the slightest cue and get results. Indeed, this is what should be sought, because we should always start small, but "get big" (as Harry puts it) only if we need to. And horses, just like people, can enjoy a run without feeling rushed and pinched inside.

Just writing this, I instantly am reminded of the difference in the way it feels to rush or to relax. There is something like a short-circuit that occurs in the mind when we prod ourselves forward beyond what

Harry working two horses, clearly in no hurry. *(Harry Whitney Collection)*

can be done in the present. Awareness of the actual moment contracts while some view of out there in the future is substituted. It robs us of the fullness of true experience in this real live moment for the promise of some artificial future we hope to achieve but never quite reach.

Perhaps worst of all is that horses only live in this present moment, but must endure our folly. No wonder they shake their heads when we go to rushing them. They don't get-on-board with our ways like an employee might for an overzealous boss. Rather, they look at us with dubious eyes and outright agitation, and surely figure we're at least nuts, and maybe even dangerous. It unfortunately robs our horses of what could be clear communication and a positive exchange, if we only would ask them things first with a simple, gentle, and unhurried request.

I know what it is to realize quite suddenly that I've been zooming around like a maniac, only then to take a deep breath and relax, letting go of some of that intensity and anxiety. If I can become conscious of this state of hurriedness in my manner before I go work with my horse, then I can make the effort to leave it behind when I approach the paddock. It is a simple thing, but the affect on the horse is profound. I sat there at Harry's and watched at least a dozen examples of rushed requests revealed to folks by the spectating clinician, and not surprisingly, every time a person asked a horse something in a calmer way, the horse's response was much less agitated.

An interesting by-product of regularly "chilling out" before going to work with a horse is that before long, I feel my body and mind automatically beginning to ease up as I begin to organize my daily duties towards getting with a horse. It starts to happen on its own as a response to facilitate the hard won conscious efforts. Going to work with a horse becomes an internal cue for me that it is time to leave the hurried constructs of this modern world back in that place, and respect the horse enough to meet him in the pasture entirely focused on him. It is a willingness to be there in that moment without time bearing down on me—not penciled in a tight thirty minute slot between a meeting and a doctor's appointment—but to be there as fully as the

What'cha hurrying for? Harry outside the round pen in Tennessee.
(Tom Moates)

dust and dung on my boots rather than with the intent (conscious or unconscious) to grab the lead and get this done so I can get to those other things that are so pressing. Horses have become too important to me to cheat them that way.

Chapter 8

(Tom Moates)

Building a Stop

Sokeri (my mare) just wouldn't stop.

Well...she sorta would, but she sorta wouldn't.

Sounds wishy-washy? Yep. Sorta sums it up exactly right.

It wasn't for lack of effort on my part, though, let me tell you.

It is rather painful to admit I could haul back on the reins and get her to stop. I sure hated to do that in a snaffle bit, but it worked to block her forward motion when nothing else would. It was a far cry from willingness and lightness. And then, less than a minute later she'd be drifting off again on her own anyway.

The situation was just lousy. Not dangerous, or bad tempered, or defiant, or terrible...just a consistently lousy flakey sorta stop that never stuck.

It is reminiscent of the trotting circles deal. In that situation for the longest time, as I explained earlier, she went to a trot without me initiating it. I tried to remedy it by blocking her forward motion with the bit, and even backing before asking for a walk again. I thought once I got things started in my direction, that then consistency in a well timed release would build increasing softness in to the deal and we'd get improvement. It never happened that way, though. Similarly in this instance, I was resorting to biceps on the bit rather than getting the thought of a stop initiated to then have the horse stop herself. She just wasn't with me by any stretch of the imagination.

My first book, *Discovering Natural Horsemanship*, even ends with a short afterword on this very note. It provides clear evidence as to how embarrassingly long this problem persisted. After triumphantly getting this mare to stand willingly when at a stop in the final chapters (and closing the story in a nice way that made me look like I'd gotten something done with her), she started inexplicably walking off again. It left me more lost than ever and wondering what to do. So I wrote the short afterword and gave the truth to my readers about this horse and the situation being not so perfect. That was several years ago. So still, here we were, in the same old trouble.

Now, I bet you're thinking it was in my release—or lack thereof—or it being improperly timed if it was there at all. And you might be right...but you might be wrong.

I will tell you I got a stop built into this horse and how it came about. I mean a real stop. A stop that the butt drops and the hind feet dig in right now at the slightest hint of my asking for it. No biceps needed nowadays. It is a stop she must enjoy giving, since it is always right there for the asking, and one that she seems comfortable with where she now stays put happily until I ask for her to move off. I can hardly believe it really. She never seemed so content before to follow my lead when stopping, and I never had the mare content to stand still for any length of time before when riding. And, as with several

Tom's "let's get down to business" look with Niji. *(Terry McCoy)*

situations involving me and a horse, it only took years to figure out and about two seconds to get going once it became clear.

Sokeri's stop is one more of the things that unfolded through my work with Harry. Harry is known for, "seeing things from the horse's point of view." This is a statement open to various interpretations, but I came to understand that these words represent an overarching approach. The phrase seeks to establish a mindset in the person to always keep a focus on how the horse is feeling and operating at any given moment. Then add to that the application of just what we might do to improve how the horse feels about things if there is a sticking point. That's boiled down, but pretty well gives the basics of the idea.

It sounds simple. I know from my own experience, from watching others, and from reading some responses to my essays though, that discussing horsemanship can be an incredibly imprecise art. It is hard to share ideas and experiences even with people that relate to humans and horses because every horse and each situation is unique. No template of horsemanship, and no cookie cutter program, can be placed onto every situation with a horse to get a dependable outcome. No special tack is going to fix a horse either, no matter how expensive it is or whose face is smiling next to it. Even when you have a breakthrough with a horse and explain it to others to the best of your ability, they may not "get it." But, I'm certain that progress can be made. That's what keeps me struggling along. Every now and then I "get it."

Which leads back to Sokeri's miserable pitiful sorta-stop, and that idea of a properly timed release. The very basic building block of any good relationship with a horse is the right release from the pressure of an "ask." It is the most obvious thing to work on at first, even though knowing or feeling when to release often eludes the human, even when trying to be critically aware of it.

I worked on the correct release for stopping from the beginning with Soke. Now, I may or may not have had the best timing, but I can say with complete confidence that I tried really hard to get it right, always. At all times when asking for a stop I remained very conscious of releasing at the right moment on the reins, as well as my focus of pressure, when Sokeri began a stop. It never stuck, though. I either had to haul back more than I wanted to on those reins, or never effect a stop, period.

I considered blaming the hard mouthed situation on whatever training the mare had before I got her five years ago. I know for certain she had been ridden in a long shanked solid bit of some kind, because I had seen some kids riding her before I bought her. They were hardly worried about releasing at the right moment, or being soft about anything. They were more like rugby players trying their hands at driving race cars (horses), and I cringed when they'd yank back on the reins to get a horse to back.

I propped that thinking up with the reasoning that I may have been off a little at times on my release, but I bet I was right-on a whole bunch of the time too...and it just didn't matter as far as continuing to get a sticky stop was concerned.

Now, as explained in my first book what worked for that little while was that when I asked for a stop and didn't get it, I'd pop her up to a trot for a little while. In other words, I made the wrong thing hard, and the right thing easy. It didn't take long at that time for Soke to decide she'd just as soon stop as go to the trouble of trotting instead. But, as I explained, after it seemed like that was going so well for awhile, it fell apart for some reason. Then, the trick wouldn't work again.

I didn't know why at the time, she refused to tell me. But now I can speculate that while making the wrong thing hard by trotting produced the desired result for awhile, it still never really got her thought with me. It really was just a cheap trick...a temporary fix because I never truly captured and maintained her attention in a really meaningful way.

Next, for several reasons that don't matter to her stop, Sokeri got to be a pasture ornament for about a year. When I gathered her up and began again with her in the round pen, many things suddenly went great, minus the stop of course. I had worked with other horses in that year while she was off, which I think gave a fresh perspective on her for me. It surely increased my experience as well, providing more tools to draw from to work with her. We quickly advanced past where we had previously been in many ways, getting to new territory like side-passing...but the stop still stunk.

I brought the stopping problem up to Harry, and this is where an interesting thing happened. I experienced a hybrid fix to a problem—half Harry's advice, and half originating from me.

Harry suggested instead of getting the mare to stop, getting her to back first. The idea is to go from forward to backing, then stop. I thought about that, and figured it was a great point. We should be able to ask most anything of our horses and expect they can do it. That might be going from the walk to the trot, going from straight into a turn at any given moment, or even a lead change...so why not going from forwards to backwards? I tried it.

I experienced some pretty crude success. Something along

the lines of: we ride forward-(I ask, okay Sokeri go backward)-we go forward another five steps-(I hang in there with the ask, backwards girl, hello!)- we stop-and finally we sluggishly move backwards-(yeah...that wasn't so great).

One thing that was new since I last worked with this mare was my expectations of horses in general, particularly of their attention. I had seen Harry ride dozens of horses, and as my own experiences mounted, I began to reflect on those memories and see for the first time that what I often witnessed Harry doing wasn't always cues for the horse to do some particular action in a mechanical way, but rather were

Carole Hess on Saymos in an arena with Bruce Lawson on Wrangler at a clinic in Virginia, playing a game where one pretends to be a cow and the other cuts. *(Terry McCoy)*

things designed to get and hold the horse's attention.

I found focus is the crux of the matter much of the time. You can't lead a horse's thought without the horse's focus. Without the horse's attention, you've got no horse. I know this sounds pretty basic, but the huge number of examples proving that so many people (and put me first on this list) don't get it, warrants its stating and repeating. I should paint this wisdom on my refrigerator door to keep it fresh in my mind!

Likewise, only if you get the horse's attention is communication possible. Next, it is time to try and see if you can get the horse to willingly move his thoughts along the direction you ask. Thoughts weigh nothing, Harry says, so if you can direct a thought it requires only the slightest effort on the person's part. Then the horse carries his own heavy self along the way of the thought.

Horses are heavy, thoughts weigh nothing. In a well tuned situation where a person directs a horse's thoughts, there is no battle, no hauling back on the reins for a stop per my difficulties with Sokeri. If Soke and I could share the idea of "stop," then I'd ask, she'd get the idea, she'd stop, and I'd never need to put any real pressure on those reins. I probably should be able to get a stop from adjusting my seat and never even going to the reins for that matter—but only if she was with me and willing.

Somewhere in the previous year I lost the wishy-washy patience of trying five thousand times to get something going with a horse that should be there. It began to dawn on me that when I go through a bunch of "phases," or whatever you want to call those graduations of pressure, when asking something of a horse, I actually built in a resistance to my requests sometimes. Instead of bringing a horse along to the right idea, it can have the effect of helping a horse learn to tune me out.

Too much "please...pretty please...okay now I mean it...alright I'm going to get big now horse...etc.," can just make a horse mentally leave the scene. They can build resistance to your requests from these graduations of pressure, and sometimes it may be best and most direct to give the horse a chance (begin where you want to end up, always), but then get to it! The attention must be on the human, and the human does well to put that attention to a more quick and definite use in some circumstances.

I found that just firming up and insisting on what I ask right at the beginning if I make a request and the horse was not attentive to me and my initial ask, that I could get the horse's true attention and be done with all that pretty-please-working-on-my-release stuff for the next five years. I found it can be better at times to get the horse on board up front, let there be no ambiguity about what's going on, and insist on the proper outcome. Then, once that short initial potentially large moment is done, the horse often follows along with very little pressure from then on. The up front firmness of a request can act to help the horse have less stress over all. One or two moments of just getting big at first to be done with trouble is way easier than weeks and months (years?) of diddling around being too soft to ever apply what is necessary to bring about results.

I remember riding a horse out on BLM land in the desert with Harry near his place one afternoon, for example. He had his hands full working with Beaumont, a mule he had just acquired at the time, from his saddle horse. I was trying to get a Quarter Horse mare to walk fast without breaking into a trot or drop back to a snail's pace. I forget

Harry works with Stoney at a horsemanship clinic in Floyd, Virginia.
(Tom Moates)

what I said about the situation as I passed by a momentarily very hectic Harry, but he replied something like, "just get that done, Tom." No advice, like I expected. No discussion about releases or some deeper horse psychoanalysis, but rather a statement saying, "get a grip, I know you can manage that—just do it."

And that's exactly what happened. Like magic, I just insisted somehow, maybe it just was enough of a boost to kick my assertiveness into drive, and the horse responded. And that was that. I never had more trouble with it that day.

Back in the round pen with Sokeri, I worked on that forward/backward deal for about five minutes. I was focusing on properly timed releases for everything, and doing my best to avoid getting into her mouth with my biceps. I thought about stopping that horse every way I could think about it for the five hundredth time. We doodled around until I had just had it.

With the split reins in my left hand and her going forward, I asked for reverse. When she kept walking I kept the slight pressure back on the reins and a slightly rocked back position in the saddle, but then added a loud SMACK! onto the leather of my shotgun chaps with the end of a rein in my right hand.

I mean to tell you, that horse woke up. Her head shot up, and she was completely attentive. She suddenly shot backwards at the slightest request on the reins. I was just as shocked at the results as she was!

We went through the new drill only once more. No graduation of phases—just one chance to back (beginning where I wanted to end up with light pressure in the reins and small seat adjustment) and then SMACK! From then on when I asked for reverse, or stop for that matter, she was right on it. If I've gone to the smack again since, it has only been a couple times at most.

It all boiled down to her attention. She seemed delighted afterwards to stop or back, and to stay put as well. This was unprecedented. It unfolded that fast, and had nothing really to do with when and how I released, but had everything to do with grabbing and holding her attention, letting her know I was serious, and following that up with the request I wanted and in an assertive way.

It was just as if she had been testing me all those years, and I'd failed the leader test. If she could tune me out easily, and knew I'd just hang in there for a bunch of graduations of pressure, I was clearly not much of a blip on her radar. Once I passed that test finally, she became confident in me, and is happy to stop and stay stopped if I like, contently and quietly.

It may be difficult to understand the distinction between moving out of fear, and moving out of willingness. That is really an area that is experiential and may not transfer to the written page. Seeing the difference has taken me quite a bit of work with Harry, and for many horse folk it may require a bunch of work to get right. But, one must strive to get a willing unbothered reaction in the horse to seek the best possible relationship.

Sokeri stops right away now, but not nervously. She isn't afraid of getting slapped around or having spurs dug in her sides (I don't even wear spurs, by the way—they aren't necessary if a horse is already willingly following the thoughts you project without mechanical manipulation) if she gets some wrong answer. Rather, she keeps her focus on me when I ride and instantly recognizes the soft request to stop and stops. If she missed it, it would be because her thoughts were elsewhere (really my fault for not recognizing it and fixing it), not because she was in any way actively defying me. Horses are not created with that ability, and never try to "get over" on a person intentionally. That dishonesty is strictly a human trait. They just "look out for number one," as Harry puts it sometimes.

This point is very, very important to understand. The chap slap that worked in this particular incident is the same kind as was used in the round pen when I first got back from Arizona. It was just a way to break into her otherwise wayward thoughts, and to have a conversation. Otherwise, if I can't access her true attention, my biceps on the bit are not only ineffective, but are so because they are nothing more than a nuisance to her. They are like a horse fly biting her hide when she is trying to think about getting to the grass on the other side of a fence. (I'm reduced to being a big horsefly up there on her back—visualize that!)

The rider entering the horse's mind as an annoyance is completely different than a horse attentively trusting and following the rider like they would a lead mare in a herd going somewhere with intention, for instance. A horse following in this situation may have no idea where that lead mare is headed, but you can bet he's going to follow, and with gusto.

To add to the confusion and be accurate, I should point out that the slap of a chap also can cause fear if used differently. So can a flag, or a coil of rope, or the human voice. That very same action alternately can bring about willingness. The difference is in the incredibly nebulous and sensitive world of equestrian feel, timing, and understanding.

It is exactly here where the rubber meets the road in horsemanship. This is where we try and often fail as we work towards getting to see, and present, things from the horse's point of view. It is also where, when we make a breakthrough and "get it," the world of the horse opens up to us and we make progress like nothing else can produce. Those golden shiny moments in the sun are worth all the rainy days, and even horsemanship hurricanes.

Chapter 9

Matter-of-Factness

Harry and I hopped on his green mule (that's a Kawasaki mule, a vehicle akin to a small truck, not a mule-mule with big floppy ears) and motored up a gravel road on his place in Salome, Arizona. We headed out to fetch two horses in a pen at one corner of his property that needed to be brought down to the arena and tacked up.

At this time I had just recently arrived from Virginia. At that point in my development as a horseman I had been around horses daily for a couple of years as a novice trying to improve, but I had logged precious little time around seasoned horse folk. I had experienced first-hand practically none of the basics one finds on a ranch or farm with working horses. At home, when I went to move horses a fair distance, it meant putting a halter and lead rope on them and walking them—even if it meant hoofing it over a mile away, which was often the case. As Harry and I rode along on the mule, I just assumed we would be walking these horses back down.

We arrived at our destination, tied halters on the horses we needed, and walked them through the gate. Harry led his ahead of me over to the mule and sat down in the driver's seat—the horse standing beside him looking around.

Yikes, I thought. Really? You're going to hold that rope out

Niji and Tom riding out around the farm in Virginia. *(Carol Moates)*

the open doorway of the vehicle while you drive and lead that horse running along side the dusty, loud, rattling mule? Obviously he was. Then suddenly it was obvious that I was going to as well, from the passenger's side. So that's what I did, acting totally cool of course, like I did it all the time and thought nothing of it.

Harry started the engine, put the mule in gear, and off we went. The horses followed along fine. They never blinked, just jogging along side of us, even with slack in the lead ropes. Harry obviously never even considered the questions in my head: "Won't this mule spook these horses? What if they pull away or slam into the mule as we travel along?"

The horses apparently never considered it either. We arrived safe and sound at our destination down by the bunkhouse and round corral, and went about the business of tacking them up.

That simple experience sticks with me and really stands out in my memory of important horse moments. It impressed me not because it was exceptional, but because it was completely un-exceptional. Not because when I got home I immediately began moving horses by holding the lead rope out of my pick up truck window saving me all kinds of time, but because of the important aspect of general horsemanship it clarified for me. Nothing short of a cornerstone of horsemanship reveled itself to me in that instant—what I now call, matter-of-factness.

I wondered after that little trip if those two horses were accustomed to this routine of running along side a vehicle with the lead rope held by a person within. Maybe Harry had desensitized them to it already?

I soon saw evidence of horses that came into Harry's place for clinics that I was pretty sure never had been introduced to this means of travel before. They got asked to lead along side the mule, and it went without any trouble. A few weeks later at home, I was armed with new confidence from being around Harry for two solid weeks and seeing how things can be with horses when handled by an experienced horseman. My curiosity about the matter was laid to rest once and for all when my own horses instantly followed along side my pickup truck with the lead rope held through the window. I knew they had never experienced this before, and I still half-expected to get my arm ripped off, but it went just flawlessly. They jogged right along with me. If I could do this, anybody could do it. I was still amazed...but well pleased.

I'm not naive enough to think no horse ever spooks at something like this. What surprised me though was that it just didn't happen in any of the cases I had witnessed. That's a 100% success rate out of at least twenty-five horses with a full range of ages and training.

The key was expectation. Harry absolutely expected the horses to behave as he wanted, and they did. I experimented with this after I noticed it. When I gave an ounce of positive expectation, I believe I got a pound of positive outcome in return that I wasn't getting before when I was preemptively trying to foresee trouble. I also realized that with Harry, it wasn't a conscious effort on his part. I bet he never thought to himself, "okay Harry, be sure to expect this horse to follow your lead...." It was just a built-in part of his way with them. It was as automatic as how he always had the left split rein over top of the right one in his hands. He never thought to sort that out, it was just authentically Harry, and as automatic to him as drawing oxygen into his lungs.

Carol and grandson, Jake, on her stallion, Chief. *(Tom Moates)*

I began to consider just how much this mindset might have to do with horses sometimes just falling in line and following a person's lead. That was something I could use more of. I suddenly became quite certain that if I always approach a horse expecting to find the next problem, that I wouldn't be let down and surely will find it, and most likely right away. But, if I approach a horse matter-of-factly, not expecting anything except a willing partner following my lead whatever it is, I may very well find that's what I get much of the time.

Trouble is obvious when it brews—it's usually pretty hard to miss. Then I can worry about it. But if I go looking for problems, maybe I actually project issues onto the horse that just wouldn't be there otherwise. Maybe I create problems for my horse.

Matter-of-factness is really giving the horse the benefit of believing in him, that he by default gets things right whenever he can.

Establishing matter-of-factness as the normal state of affairs in the relationship makes the right thing no-big-deal. You are telling your horse, "yeah, nice day, huh?" as you go about your business.

This has two effects. First, it means working without nurturing disbelief in the horse, and therefore not breathing life into a belief that I expect him to mess up whatever I am setting out to do, even before it happens. Second, it also has the by product of not giving him some great round of praise for the basic stuff he should be doing all the time anyway. The horse deserves that regularity of just work-a-day evenness. Expect him to get in the trailer, and don't be surprised when he does. Expect him to stand when you mount, and don't be surprised when he does. And don't give him a blue ribbon every time he does either...he should be able to do those things.

I asked Harry about this idea--my matter-of-factness theory-- although much later than my trip to Arizona. It was well after reflecting on it and experimenting with it at home in several circumstances over the course of many months. I pointed out the above mule leading experience as the example to him, since he had been with me on that one.

"The horse should follow the feel on the lead rope, no matter where it comes from...or where it goes," he responded.

That's matter-of-factness, exactly, I thought. Harry simply confirmed that, regardless of the circumstances, the horse should follow your lead. That "should" is an optimistic attitude in motion, which comes across from the human to the horse as communication in the form of feel, posture, and actions. The true belief that the horse should follow your feel...period, changes you. It should never be the justification for punishment when he doesn't. It is, rather, the powerful tool of unconscious confidence. The horse reads this. It makes a difference. It is itself an approach to working with your horse. It can be developed in a person.

I don't believe Harry ever even remotely considered the horses that day in Salome might have had an issue with following along beside the mule. That was very different from my mindset at the time, which was more along the lines of, "The mule is noisy, what if this horse goes berserk? What if...?"

What-if-ness is the opposite of matter-of-factness.

This doesn't mean go to sleep when handling your horse. Of

Harry and Tom riding out in the Arizona desert. *(Harry Whitney Collection)*

course it doesn't mean forget what you need to be safe and aware around a horse, as anyone should clearly realize when considering what I'm saying here. It means to stay glass half full in your attitude about the horse and avoid creating problems for horses by bringing along doubt, indecision, and hesitation to your work with them.

The "what ifs" are a way to beg for trouble—to kind of see if you can find problems, or even actually ask for them. A timid moment in your thinking can change the horse happily following your lead into one skeptical of his leader. Matter-of-factness helps keep the seeds of confusion from ever being sown.

If you have a question in your mind, the horse is probably going to have a question in his too. If you have only an answer in your mind, even if the horse has a question in his, he's likely just as happy to go with the answer you're already presenting.

Chapter 10

(Tom Moates)

Riding the Line

The level of constant support a horse needs from the rider, especially a green horse, completely eluded me.

It amounted to no little passing insight when I began to figure this out. Rather, it quickly proved to be a profound earthquake of realization. The pillars shook on which my skills with horses were unknowingly quite precariously placed. No wonder they had occasion to tumble down (and for me to tumble off a horse).

Oddly, years of sustained attention to detail during ground work and when riding still left this insight laying beyond the scope of anything I ever recognized or guessed. I thought I paid very close attention to the horses I worked with. In a way, surely I did—I watched hard and looked for meaning in the way the horses handled themselves.

I saw ears and eyes giving signals. I thought a horse was with me when we rode along easily in the direction I chose. I thought getting a horse to willfully circle at my command meant focus was on me. Yet, there were mammoth holes in my abilities to truly get and hold a horse's attention. There existed a chasm in the support I offered a horse big enough to drive a combine through.

Until fairly recently, I possessed no clue of snowballing trouble in the horses I rode until the progression became all too evident. At that point, when the horse is plainly pushing through my requests and on his own line of action, the results were all too late to fix. The roots of problems remained unobserved, but I sure noticed wrecks and fights and bad mis-behavior, and I worked to sort that stuff out. To put it another way, if the progression of trouble was scaled 1 to 10, I'd see a 9 or 10 and never come close to seeing a 5 or 6. But, I needed to be able to see that 1 to best support the horse and get him feeling completely right about things. Not to mention making my life a whole lot more pleasant and safe.

Substantial gains in progress certainly were made on many fronts in my work with horses. If not, I surely would have quit...

or spontaneously combusted. Not to mention that all the previous chapters in this book wouldn't be here either. The joys of breaking through to a new understanding all along the horsemanship journey are incredibly exciting and strong motivation to continue the work.

I sorted out some troubles, learned much, advanced my understanding of how horses tick, and saw some great positive changes at times. I even rode some horses in paddocks, round pens, and out on the farm with seemingly good progress. Just as I'd think everything looked fantastic, they'd explode in my face. Or, I'd find my face in the dirt after a wreck, wondering how I managed to get thrown through the windshield again? How perplexing that became! I became better at crisis management than noticing and defusing the smaller escalating aspects of trouble brewing in horses that ultimately result in big trouble.

Years of working constantly with horses, consciously attempting to improve my horsemanship skills, still didn't produce in me the awareness of the depth of responsibility that goes into each moment of interacting with a horse...each moment! I even was fond of thinking about the "attention span" of a horse, but my own severely lacked—I just didn't know it. The truth is, a great many (if not 99 point 9999 percent) of my predicaments originated long before the obvious dilemmas I noticed.

It's as if there were piles of nails littered about my driveway and I clearly recognized the recurrent flat tires but didn't see the nails scattered around. Then I changed the flat, and drove on the nails again, just to get another flat, and so on. A person like me in reality would discover the nails stuck in the tire, and yet with a horse I may wonder quite awhile about those significant predicaments before paying attention to the bigger picture and focusing on the less obvious source of trouble that has cost so much for so long. Then, finally seeing the stupid problem, forever realize how ridiculous the situation was.

Harry said to me recently when referring to the light bulb illuminating over my head regarding the moment-to-moment support of the horse, "When you can't see it, you can't see it...then when you see it, you wonder how you never saw it before."

How true.

Niji became the best teacher I could ever ask for on this point... I could have choked that sorrel gelding on many occasions.

He's my wife's horse (which I'm apt to point out when he acts up). He's also the first horse I ever became closely acquainted with. Carol's sudden decision to get him, and to begin educating me on horses in general as a byproduct, sparked this unquenchable equestrian obsession that's been blazing in me ever since—poor unsuspecting spouse!

Niji is one of the usual suspects for many of my more lively essays. With him I've been, among other things, bucked off up a hill, bucked off down a hill, thrown over his head into the woods, and sling-shotted under an oak board fence full speed, broken cinch, saddle, and all. Each time afterwards he seems to be standing right there looking down at me like, "What you doing down there?" Followed instantly by, "Oh look, there's some grass over there...." Such a partner.

Carol has a wonderful little Appaloosa gelding now named Stoney. His leopard pattern is incredible, and I never tire of gazing on the pattern of black spots that just cover this horse head to tail. She has been riding him for about six months, and he is much more steady and dependable in his training than Niji. So, I've devoted my attention to

Niji lately since he'd been just freeloading in a paddock by the house for awhile. Truth be known, our thorny past lured me to it as well—I couldn't resist seeing if I could get things going better than before.

Still we wound up in the same old circle of trouble. Literally, years passed before I realized I missed dozens of little things before the bigger problems reared their ugly heads in a clearly obvious way. It's hard to say how many times we started over from the beginning. Ground work, saddle, round pen, paddock, outside the gate...catastrophic failure! This closed loop played many revolutions.

The plan always is to get Niji going so I can ride him to check and feed the other horses on this farm and another close by. Not to mention to simply be able to ride him on the trail and in the world in general.

Finally, in this most recent go around, there came a clear phase where I finally recognized I missed things ahead of the trouble that arose. I still couldn't isolate and understand what they were, but at least I knew they existed. It is like those scientists that know something exists out in space that they can't see, but they can see its gravitational affect on other heavenly bodies that are observable. Niji's gravitational affect on my heavenly body completely convinced me finally that something I couldn't see was definitely there close by and affecting me!

That's when I asked Carol and another capable friend, our horse hoof trimmer, Terrie Wood, to come over to the paddock and watch me ride Niji.

I knew from experience that one particular spot in the paddock brought out the recurrent trouble that Niji and I always confronted.

In the past, our issues manifested when we left the confines of the corral and got out onto the farm roads. To make several long stories short, usually the first trip went pretty well. Then, at some point along the way, usually the second time out, I'd notice Niji become less willing to go where I wanted. Finally, things deteriorated into a huge battle where he wanted to go one way and I another, and we spun circles where I tried desperately yet futilely to pressure and release him to my idea. Eventually it led to my dismounting and walking him back home for safety.

He detoured so off my desired path during our heated debates that we were too close to barbed wire, or he'd be completely off the road, or over a ditch and up a hill, and it proved just horrendous. It caught me off guard every time (stupid human) since I always thought I'd worked through it this time, having started over from the beginning back at home.

Quite a bit of the puzzle unfolded after Carol and Terrie watched me ride. The paddock where I rode is constructed of two parts, one roundish and the other long, straight, and skinny with an open gate between them. It would resemble a key hole if seen from above. Often I rode Niji around in the circular part like it was a round pen. Then I'd ask him to straighten out and go up a slight hill, through the gate, and down the straight stretch. As we straighten out to head for the gate, he very often decided otherwise, and pushed out to the left.

This is exactly the kind of thing that always happened to ruin our rides out in the world. Once it started, it always escalated to the point of being terminal. My tendency then was to block the turn (and hopefully the thought of turning) by holding the right rein. It usually ended up with him pushing right through my block while I just held the pressure there using the bicep and waited for him to finally give in, and then release. Well, I got varying results, but none that ever fixed the dilemma. I remained so sure that the whole pressure and release reasoning was sound, though. Just like when I kept trying it for the

Tom rides a Quarter Horse mare in Arizona. *(Harry Whitney Collection)*

whole not-stopping business with Sokeri discussed earlier.

I eventually became convinced that pressure and release as I tried to apply it here was not the answer to gaining a horse's attention once he's so far gone. It may help build a nice response once the horse is with you, but as far as gaining a horse's thoughts and being consequential to them in the first place (and on a continuing basis), this horse showed me that the technique was worthless as I used it. It became one of those insane deals, as Carol says: trying the same thing over and over again expecting a different result that never comes.

So, with Carol and Terrie leaning on the fence and watching, I rode Niji a little and then predicted the future. "When we ride out towards the gate, he'll want to go left," I said.

Sure enough, he obliged. They chatted and I rode back down. Then we agreed that Terrie would call out when she saw the horse's thought leave me. It shocked me how far before the noticeable trouble area she spoke up. Hardly two steps into moving at all, let alone near the spot where Niji pushed left, Terrie called out.

She indicated he left the scene mentally while we were still straight, so I asked for a bend to the left (his favorite direction) and disengaged the hind quarters to check on his mental status. It didn't go very well. Then Terrie suggested I hold that rein until I see his thought come through to the direction I asked for. There is a difference between him moving his hind end over, and doing it with his thought also moving around as well. It is a little complicated to get figured out at first, believe me.

When I started to ask for the bend to turn, I realized I saw some of this scenario indicated in his eye. Even when his head came around to the request of my rein, if his thought remained hard back the other direction, the white of his eye that faced me was visible. This seemed to be a clear indication of his mind being in another place.

With Carol and Terrie providing further observations from their vantage point, I grew completely aghast to find out that with every step or two, Niji left me mentally. I knew I lost the mental trail earlier than when we reached the big trouble, but I never guessed just how much support it required to keep this horse on board with me mentally!

Before, what I considered to be a horse willfully following my lead as we rode ten steps calmly and happily, instead was really nothing more than Niji going where he wanted to go. I just happened to be up on his back and wanting to go to the same place by coincidence. Then, when I asked for something different, his mind was long gone elsewhere, and he wasn't real happy about changing it. In truth, I lost him nine steps ago and possessed no idea that the horse really was on his own all that time. Talk about being delusional.

Harry points out in instances like these that the importance of such matters is of enormous proportions to the horse. To us, sitting atop the horse in a round pen and asking him to turn doesn't seem like much. But Harry works hard to get the point across that to the horse a sudden unsupported moment creates a mental vacuum that can at times even seem life threatening.

That horse, in his mind, lacks any choice but to make decisions when he feels the human drop out. It is his survival instinct. In a horse like Niji, it is very strong. If he notices lack of guidance, he needs to take care of number one, and he does so by making his own decisions. If you missed the point when that change occurred, it's not the horse's fault. It's the human's. Just because I, the human, can't see it doesn't mean it isn't real. If the human can be made to see it, though, then he can work to improve the situation. We're back to the, "When you can't see it, you can't see it...then when you see it, you wonder how you never saw it before," deal.

I started to ride after that sideline help by checking in with Niji every step or two. Literally, I advanced a step and lifted one rein a little to see if his head gave to the ask instantly. If it did, I dropped the rein and went on to the next step. If his mind was elsewhere and not right there available to my request, then I worked to bring his head around and disengage the hind quarters until his thought came around too. You would not believe how lousy this went at first, and how long it took before I got four steps without him checking out on me. It took me years to get him this messed up, so I reckon I shouldn't be surprised it took quite a bit of time to get it going better.

After a couple of weeks of daily riding this way, I strung five or six steps together with him focused on me the whole time. Then I remembered something from a month earlier that I discussed with Harry. The seeds for this connection were planted when I spent a couple of days with him during his annual clinics at Mendin' Fences Farm in Tennessee, hosted by Linda Bertani and Vic Thomas. In the arena there while riding a Paso Fino, I noticed how Harry kept the horse moving—not just moving, but guided and moving forward with absolute purpose as if by some inner guidance system. I asked about this from the fence.

"I'm riding a line," Harry replied.

He explained he visualizes a line leading out in front of the horse showing the way he expects to go. Sometimes the line is straight, as if heading for a spot in the distance, like a fence post. Other times,

Tom on Niji trying to ride a line in a round pen. *(Pam Talley Stoneburner)*

the line curves and the horse arcs right along with it. As he rode, he spoke about changing the direction of the line, and the horse instantly reacted accordingly to illustrate the point.

Harry rides a line, I remembered. A line is unbroken. Ride a line with a horse and there is not a single point at which the support breaks from the human, or it wouldn't be a line. Aha!

Once I got those five or six steps together where Niji remained with me the whole way, I realized then what I'd done. I built up these multiple attentive steps in succession and strung together enough to be riding a Harry-type of line.

It's amazing that if you can't see it, you can't see it...then when you see it, you wonder how you never saw it before. This is a great example of how going to a clinic and attempting to learn sometimes unfolds to you later if you keep trying to improve with horses. It is potentially the best and most lasting form of learning there is when your own experiences bring you to a realization which is then corroborated by solid teaching you've had, but didn't have the personal reference for, until now.

I dug back through my journal entries from the Tennessee clinic and found this written: "I want to remember Harry's talk about riding a line. Actually visualizing a line that the horse tracks. This is a concrete means of removing all ambiguity from just where you expect the horse to go."

Many examples come to mind of past conversations I've heard between horse people where the discussion of horsemanship turns to the point of "just riding a horse." It becomes increasingly evident to me that the romantic vision of just hopping in a saddle and mindlessly riding the trail is just a romantic dream. It takes a huge amount of effort to get a horse to the point of riding a line, if you're me. When I finally get something that resembles it, the last thing I want to do then is drop the ball.

When one advances to a point where the horse is truly following the human's lead mentally, and the horse hasn't been let down by the person providing no place for the thoughts he now volunteers to go to, then one rides a line. A togetherness is experienced between the horse and human.

It is, however, never a human la-la-land, where our minds can check out for ten minutes, talking to a friend riding along with us or looking at shapes in the clouds on a gorgeous afternoon. We can do such things if we remain aware of supporting the horse along the trail the entire time. It is equestrian multi-tasking. When it becomes too much to keep track of though, then stick to the horse and forget that other stuff.

If we apply ourselves to the task of getting better with horses in the way Harry teaches, then we commit to supporting them. We dig around and discover their discomforts. Then we actively alter things so the horse really feels better inside. He lets go of some thoughts he previously held tightly to and allows us the trust to guide those thoughts to a different application. It brings about positive change, but is likewise a huge responsibility.

I missed this for a long time. Riding a hundred yards without trouble is not the same as riding a line a hundred yards without trouble. I completely lied to Niji when I told him I wanted his attention at first while we rode along, but then to him, I checked out and he had to assume control again for his own well being.

This can't be. If it is, it shows up in bigger and bigger ways, as with Niji and me, guaranteed. I didn't mean for it to be this way, but good intentions don't fill in the gap for the horse. The horse requires the real deal. So much needed to transpire before I could see this much. It really helped when I got a deeper look into riding a line. But, that still remained a stone in the pathway to another deeper insight. Riding the line is on the way to getting a horse with you.

Chapter 11

(Terry McCoy)

The Razor's Edge

One must, I've learned from being around Harry, often push a horse right up to the very razor's edge of going beyond his limits to cope with a troubling situation to bring about a lasting positive change. It sometimes takes urging a horse towards the very situation that is known to cause anxiety to be able to show a different and more positive way to experience the disquieting condition. This experience may be essential to pushing a horse through to a better place.

One can't really work through a horse's difficulties if the difficulties aren't right there to be worked on. Horses live in the moment, so you have to be in the middle of the occurrence to change how the horse feels about it. By getting to a better place, I mean a lasting lack of apprehension when the horse confronts the formerly difficult stimulus, whatever it was.

At the recent clinic in Virginia, Loreli, a mare owned by Rita Riddile (and her husband, Andy, who also came that week to audit), was terrified of fluttery things and got to a much better space through some help orchestrated by Harry. He gathered a team of us with flags, and some of the time I also had the dreadful piece of long blue foam insulation that Carol calls a noodle, to work various ways over several days with this mare.

Loreli was troubled by fluttery things, as many horses are, but she had a particularly strong reaction to things above her head. A person just sitting on the top of a fence panel near her, for instance, really bothered her.

I first met Loreli in Tennessee at Harry's clinic there earlier that year. She was rather explosive around flags. I'd seen her rip the lead rope out of Rita's hands and need to run off when her experience of pressure from a flag became too great. I'd seen some improvement in this at the earlier clinic, particularly when Harry had me hold her lead rope through a fence panel and at about fifteen feet distant, he gently moved from one of her eyes to the other—that is, with her behind facing Harry, he moved right to left and back until she would see him

Rita riding Loreli in Virginia. *(Terry McCoy)*

in one eye and then the other. It proved quite tough for her, and she nearly bolted quite a few times. She managed to hang in there, though, and even in a short time she began to progress substantially.

The mare at the Virginia clinic had much improved since Tennessee. Rita made clear advancements in the interim few months with her. It interested me a great deal that for such substantial spookiness, this was a horse that seemed easily ridden. Rita saddled up and rode just fine—by my standards, anyway. It is curious to me that if the horse is worried by someone on a fence panel, why not a rider up there on her back?

Anyway, back in Virginia, Loreli experienced trouble with the person on the fence scenario, and still from the flags as well. Harry gathered a bunch of us in attendance there to get up on the fence of the round pen. Loreli, excessively unconvinced about this, was led up close to us and given the chance for her own curiosity to convince her to check us out. We petted her on the face for her efforts. Before long, she became less dubious, and started to warm up pretty well to it all.

Soon came a similar operation with flags. We began on top of the fence spread out around the round pen holding flags one day early in the week. Soon we were able to get onto the ground inside the corral, and eventually begin to touch her with the flags. By the end of the week, a whole herd of us stood close together in a tight gauntlet of flags through which she easily and calmly walked or stood.

Loreli overcoming fear of folks on the fence. *(Terry McCoy)*

What a huge change! It seemed a life-altering positive change for this mare, but there were times as we approached her with flags while working on this trouble where one could just see her right at that razor's edge, about to leave the scene. She never bolted like in Tennessee, but anyone could see many times that just one additional speck of pressure and she would have had to run away, or over us, or through us. The instinct to flee was so close...but she made it through to an incredibly better place inside herself. The change came on gradually, but over a couple days it proved absolutely profound and she became a great deal improved.

It seems certain Rita left that clinic with a horse in way better shape to handle some of the things that most bothered her before. But, as Rita pointed out several times, we "tortured" her poor horse. Funny, but ironically so because it is somewhat accurate. Humans may need to torture the poor horses with what most worries them to provide them the greatest relief from these things in life. I should add, though, that if one isn't fluent in this kind of horse interaction, a horse can go over the edge and it will make things much worse. Spooked horses often harm themselves and/or others as their brains and bodies hit flight mode completely and reflexively. So realize this example is just presented to show one time where I witnessed a very capable horseman lead a group to help a horse that illustrates perfectly pushing the horse to the edge to break new ground to a better place. It is not some exercise to try on every horse, and knowing when to advance or retreat approaching a horse with something spooky is a very tricky business.

To witness a horse try that hard to get through something, for me, is quite stunning and equally as moving. That horse worked so hard mentally that you could see her eyes and ears tightly focused figuring out what to do, and her whole body, at first taut and ripply with flight and worry, really relax when she finally got to a place where she knew in her mind for certain that things there were going to be alright for her. It is the kind of observation I'll never forget. It was just so sincere a moment for the horse, and the humans really helped out that time.

Loreli works with Harry to overcome Pam Stoneburner's scary umbrella.
(Terry McCoy)

That situation is similar to one Carol worked with Stoney and the blue noodle that I witnessed. When she approached him with it, he went crazy to back away from it. Then, as is so often the case when I see Harry flag a horse for the first time, which seems totally counter intuitive to me, as soon as she'd get in there close and touch him with the thing, he'd instantly start to show relief. Before long, as she stroked him with it, he'd not only settle down, but even begin to associate comfort with the noodle. The noodle, or whatever spooky thing it is, can be way worse for the horse if it is close but unfelt. It seems to me that a weird thing touching me would be more worrisome, but it just isn't so with a horse.

The horse is an experiential creature. He can't read a book like a human, and thereby know better than to do something he shouldn't, like run out in traffic or be afraid of fluttery plastic. His instincts help him in some ways, but can hurt him too--and these are commingled with the memory of experiences. These combine to make up his demeanor. The human, therefore, must prove to the horse in real time that things are alright where the horse is convinced that they are not.

You can't show a horse a chart about trailer loading with some statistics and guidelines and expect him to understand it and then feel confidence about loading. No, you've got to get a trailer and work that horse so he enters it. At first, it might be just terrible, especially if it has been proven to the horse through experience that trailer loading is a very, very terrifying thing. Then, if a capable horse person can see

Loreli works through the gauntlet. *(Terry McCoy)*

when the horse thinks he's about to die, and prove that he won't, and start reinforcing those positive moments of clarity, eventually one gets a horse that trailer loads with confidence.

These are examples of what you encounter on the way towards getting a horse with you....

Chapter 12

(Terry McCoy)

With-You-Ness

"With-you-ness," is a 100% completely original Harry Whitney-ism.

Now, I've coined a few phrases in my time. They often result from a little artistic license applied within the act of writing, like the example in this book of the phrase, "matter-of-factness." However, I can claim no credit for the research and development of with-you-ness.

The term debuted for me just a couple of weeks ago. Finally, for the first time, I attended one of Harry's clinics with a horse from home and participated as a rider. This recent clinic was where I first heard him use the new expression.

It proved to be a miracle I ended up at the clinic at all, really. For a range of pretty formidable and pressing reasons, I resigned myself to the fact that Carol and I would not be able to make that clinic. Carol, however, lined it up for me to attend it. What a great wife! She ended up being in California visiting our youngest daughter, Mariah, at the time, and so did not get to be there herself.

Bruce and Shannon Lawson hosted it at their place, Galloping Acres, in Hanover, Virginia, about four hours from our home. I trailered Carol's sorrel gelding, the infamous Niji, up there to ride. That horse stood out as the obvious choice for me to take from the herd here since I mostly rode him at this time. Plus, we had worked hard on a ton of stuff lately. Carol rode Stoney, her leopard Appaloosa gelding these days like I mentioned earlier, since he didn't exhibit some of the sticky points Niji threw out on occasion.

Niji, as it turned out, was an absolutely perfect example of with-you-ness at the clinic. The flawlessness of his example was due to the fact that he likewise provided the wonderfully instructive juxtaposition to with-you-ness (and my own variation of the Harry-ism in the spotlight here), "not-with-me-ness."

First, let me back up and give you exactly what Harry said

about with-you-ness. Straight from him, it is defined as:

A way of the horse and human each responding to the other while participating in the same experience--both aware of, and being sensitive to, the mental desires, emotional balance, as well as physical needs of the other, during which time there is no fear, anxiety, resistance, or resentment.

Harry working with Abigale on with-you-ness. *(Pam Talley Stoneburner)*

"Pitiful!" Harry said to me. "Just pitiful!"

Such encouragement from a teacher, let me tell you! Of course, I laughed--but only because it was true.

Niji and I were in the outdoor arena with four or five other horses that were being ridden. The weather turned cold, windy, and rainy that day, so we all agreed to do a group ride in the arena since the footing remained pretty decent there, and the round pen located down the hill was a bit soupy. This way we all got in some clinic time with our horses for the day.

Already earlier that week, on the very first day of the clinic, Niji went bizerkers in the round pen. Harry got in there with him, and the gelding just ran circles a hundred miles an hour on the fence, even kicking out towards Harry in the center.

"We really are way past this," I thought to myself watching things unfold with the other spectators. Niji had been worked every way but upside down in a round pen at least a billion times, so the experience of being worked in one was nothing new. At that moment, no one had asked him to do anything more than just check in with a human. Heck, I didn't even make it into the round pen when leading the horse before things were melting down with him.

Still, he really didn't do this at home (usually, anyway). Of course, at home I was careful not to push the situation to get him to an overly challenging state of mind most of the time. I didn't tiptoe around him in how I handled the horse, don't get me wrong. Rather, I would work in locations that became safe havens. In them, I could do most anything I needed to while keeping a watchful eye on where Niji's mind was. There were no other pressing, competing, or extraordinary stimuli in these very static environments. I figured that was the best approach. I sought, after all, a calm horse feeling peachy about stuff inside himself.

I watched this fire breathing dragon snorting and about to consume Harry in the round corral there for a few minutes. I began to consider that maybe instead of creating a horse that felt good about things inside, like me or some poor clinician asking something of him, what I had produced was an external world wherein he could feel good inside at those moments because I rarely challenged his need to decide whether to keep a thought with me or take control of it back.

Here at the clinic, in this strange place, with horses everywhere, there was no avoiding the challenging parts of horse life any way you sliced it. Push came to shove all over the place there, which didn't happen in the artificial reality I'd constructed at home. He felt the need to assume control of his situation. It was pretty vigorous mental and physical control he wished to assert, at that.

This example is a perfect one of classic NOT-with-you-ness. This was just like Sokeri in the round pen with the chap slap after I got back from Arizona all those chapters ago. But, I knew about that stuff now. I could work a horse to a better spot in the round pen (I thought, anyway). Still, here before me galloped a running, kicking, snorting, embarrassing example of not-with-you-ness.

At home, I'd ridden Niji daily. I'd gone through the challenges spelled out last chapter as we began riding the line. Getting around in and out of the paddock, yard, and round pen was pretty easy and fun these days. I easily opened gates from him, for instance—the same two gates all the time, but still! There are some challenging front and hind end control matters that go on in there, some desensitizing to the clanging metal swinging gate bouncing up against him, and so on.

Once opened, I often liked to trot him up to an open gate, swing him around, back through the gate, get the hindquarters disengaged around again, and then trot him off. I really felt positive about this kind of progress. I never could have strung so many maneuvers together into such a cohesive flowing whole before. And, I was keeping in mind his attitude, making sure his head was low and he seemed otherwise relaxed as well while I worked at our advancements. I noticed when he seemed to begin to show trouble or mental resistance, and worked to stay well ahead of it. This was certainly evolution in our development, but the menacing and sinister truth was that it did not necessarily fit the whole bill under the heading of with-you-ness.

If I can easily and without resistance approach an open gate, back the horse through it, then turn and trot off at home with Niji willfully following my lead, I might think of that as with-you-ness. At that moment, to me, it might actually represent a decent microcosmic view of with-you-ness. But, if I can not even get him to simply walk along with me to the round pen on a lead rope before he loses it when we are somewhere else, I'd be lying if I claimed that horse was truly with me.

There is no openness in the horse's mind at that point looking to me for guidance, input, or comfort. If anything, I represent an increasing nuisance as he tries to sort out and command what needs to be done in this new situation for his self preservation. Is it any wonder I can't get Niji consistent enough at home to ride him to feed the other horses once I head out onto the farm road? It doesn't matter how many times I go back to the beginning and start over. I can go through the basic maneuvers from ground work to round pen to riding out a million times, and none of it makes any difference without with-you-ness in the deeper sense. If I don't have that horse with me everywhere, I don't have with-you-ness.

The lesson here for me, as I closely considered Harry's new term, was that with-you-ness is not the least bit about what I can do with a horse. It doesn't make any difference if I can rope cows off of him or piaffe perfectly or back through a gate. This point became brutally clear to me pretty quickly that day. It is, rather, about what the horse does when things get tight that matters, no matter what action is sought.

With-you-ness transcends a nice relaxed response of the horse to cues. With-you-ness gets down to the very deep level of relationship where the horse and human, "each respond to the other while participating in the same experience--both aware of, and being sensitive to, the mental desires, emotional balance, as well as physical needs of the other, during which time there is no fear, anxiety, resistance, or resentment," per Harry's definition.

This means, the two are on the same page at the same moment when approaching a new round pen. If a tiger hops out of a tree on the way there, and that horse is with you at that moment looking for what to do next...now that's true with-you-ness. It's also an over-exaggeration. Maybe not a tiger, but say one of those petrifying, horse eating plastic grocery bags comes blowing by. Or, a dog shows up out of the blue yipping about the horse's feet. That stuff can happen anytime, and if we get better and better at working with our horses, hopefully we can achieve this state of with-you-ness where rider and horse face those threats together as one. If you think about it, it seems to be something every rider should seriously consider with any horse.

Niji just being in that round pen running around bonkers with Harry is no different than any other pushing of his comfort zone. That's where the work to be done is to be found—the work I'd been doing to avoid it was just the opposite of what needed to happen.

But I digress quite a bit...what I started to share some time ago was that Niji and I were in the outdoor arena with four or five other horses being ridden at the clinic. Niji was saddled up, but I remained on the ground at this point. His rope halter was still on, with a twenty foot lead line attached. After the round pen episode earlier in the week, I figured a little ground work was in order before mounting up. He entered fine, and seemed pretty "with me" leading in. All the action in that arena, not to mention horses in pastures on two different fences, took its toll quickly and completely. That horse lost it. He violently shook his head and took off.

I maintained a grip on the lead rope, but only after taking many vigorous yanks Niji inflicted upon me. Again, with another fantastic example, Niji helps us to better understand with-you-ness by showing complete and utter not-with-me-ness. I went to get big with him once he blew past the initial spazz out. I simply seemed unable to get his attention. In fact, and a little embarrassing, I cracked my left knee attempting to get big enough to be of any consequence to the gelding at this point, and limped over to Harry. So this is where the clinician entered the picture, took the lead rope, and said, "Pitiful! Just pitiful!"

Harry got big, and wasted no time capturing and maintaining Niji's attention. As said in a previous chapter, without the horse's attention, you got no horse. So that needs to be in place before anything like with-you-ness can form. Before long, I sat on the sidelines watching a changed Niji carefully watching Harry.

Harry mounted up. He rode the gelding for a little while. What all transpired there wouldn't necessarily work with another horse anyway, so it is far less important than the fact that Harry's work had the cumulative effect of gaining and holding the horse's attention. Before long, that horse was moving forward like he had somewhere

Pitiful! Just Pitiful! *(Terry McCoy)*

to go—and right now. And he did. Harry had him riding a line to somewhere, and he felt purpose with every step. He was with Harry. His thoughts no longer bounced around like mad, but willfully and happily focused to a task.

There is a singular pleasure in getting on a horse you have spent forever working with immediately after Harry has ridden him. Harry dismounted and I hopped up there, and it was like nothing before or since. It is trifling, because you can't get it working that well yourself. Yet, it is profoundly helpful to experience what can be done with your own horse in a short time if the right feel, timing, and other miraculous things are applied well.

And that's as good as it's gotten.

With-you-ness is still in the experimental phase for this horseman. I've had glimpses to share in these examples, but any more answers unfortunately I don't possess, at least not yet. Niji and I are back home, and at a much different place than when we left for the clinic. When I ride him now, we move. We move like we mean it, riding that line to somewhere important, even if it is just down the paddock or around the round pen. That's different, fine, and fun.

But now, I'm experiencing all kinds of new trouble in getting him to disengage his hind quarters, especially to the right. His thoughts aren't coming around that way. Before, we didn't have this trouble—his butt came around back then, even when his thoughts didn't, I guess. Now, I have to really wait for the thoughts and the butt. He stalls terribly, flounders around, and this shows where that horse isn't with me now.

Or, maybe I've missed the release earlier on when working at this deal and created the new trouble? Or maybe he's stepping his front end over ahead of disengaging the hind, and I have to now figure out how to sort this out, and when and what to release for? I'm just not sure.

So there you have it. The elusive with-you-ness. Whatever it is, like feel, if you get it, you'll be seriously getting things working with your horse. Maybe then, you'll let me know what it is? At the very least, I'll keep plodding along trying to get it sorted out....

Harry riding Niji, working on gaining some with-you-ness. *(Terry McCoy)*

(Harry Whitney)

About the Author

Tom Moates is a leading equestrian journalist and author. This award winning writer is on the mastheads of *Equus* and *Horse Connection* magazines as a Contributing Writer, where his work frequently appears. Articles he pens run in many major horse magazines in the United States and abroad including *The American Quarter Horse Journal, Eclectic-Horseman, I. M. Cowgirl, British Horse, America's Horse, Paint Horse Journal, Western Horseman,* and *Hoofbeats* (Australia). *Discovering Natural Horsemanship*, his first book, is firmly established as a staple of modern equestrian literature. He lives on a solar powered farm with his wife Carol and a herd of horses in the Blue Ridge Mountains of Virginia.

CPSIA information can be obtained
at www.ICGtesting.com
Printed in the USA
BVHW04s1509220418
513843BV00005B/92/P